GROKKING ALGORITHM

BLUEPRINT

Effective Methods and Functions
of Grokking Algorithms

WILLIAM TURNER

Table of Contents

Introduction 1

Chapter 1: Role of Algorithms in Computing....................2

Algorithms as a Technology..................................... 6

Chapter 2: Getting Started 12

Insertion Sort... 12

Analyzing Algorithms.. 15

Chapter 3: Recurrences and Function Growth...................21

The Recurrences Substitution Method 21

Growth of Functions... 25

Designing Algorithms.. 27

Chapter 4: Randomized Algorithms and Probabilistic Analysis ...32

Randomized Algorithms 32

Probabilistic Analysis 36

Chapter 5: Quicksort 42

Randomized Quicksort Algorithm 44

Real-Life Examples... 46

Analysis of Quicksort 50

Chapter 6: Heapsort...54

Real-Life Example of Heapsort 58

Maintaining the Heap Property 61

Chapter 7: Linear Time Sorting **64**

Chapter 8: Order Statistics and Medians **73**

Order Statistics 73

Selection in Worst-Case Linear Time 76

Chapter 9: Hash Tables **80**

Hashing Collisions 81

Direct-Address Tables 84

Perfect Hashing 87

Chapter 10: Elementary Data Structures **93**

Stacks and Queues 93

Representing Rooted Trees 98

Implementing Pointers and Objects 100

Linked Lists 103

Chapter 11: Binary Search Trees **106**

Querying a Binary Search Tree 110

Chapter 12: Red-Black Trees **115**

Red-Black Trees Specific Properties 118

Chapter 13: Data Structures Augmentation **123**

Dynamic Order Statistics 128

Chapter 14: Dynamic Programming **134**

Elements of Dynamic Programming 138

Chapter 15: Greedy Algorithms 142

    Elements of the Greedy Strategy 146

Conclusion 151

References 152

Introduction

The book Grokking Algorithms: Effective methods and functions of Grokking Algorithms (a part of the 'Grokking' series) is a great resource for anyone who wants to understand algorithms and the different methods used to solve problems. The book explains how these algorithms work, with real-life examples, making it easy to grasp the basic concepts. The logical sequence of chapters enhances learning and retains essential information in long-term memory for a better understanding of algorithms and proper application of functions that implement those algorithms. It also helps develop problem-solving skills.

If you want to start grokking algorithms, this book is for you. It is a detailed guide to understanding the world of complex mathematical computations. This book will help you better understand how algorithms work and how to apply them effectively in your daily life.

Chapter 1

Role of Algorithms in Computing

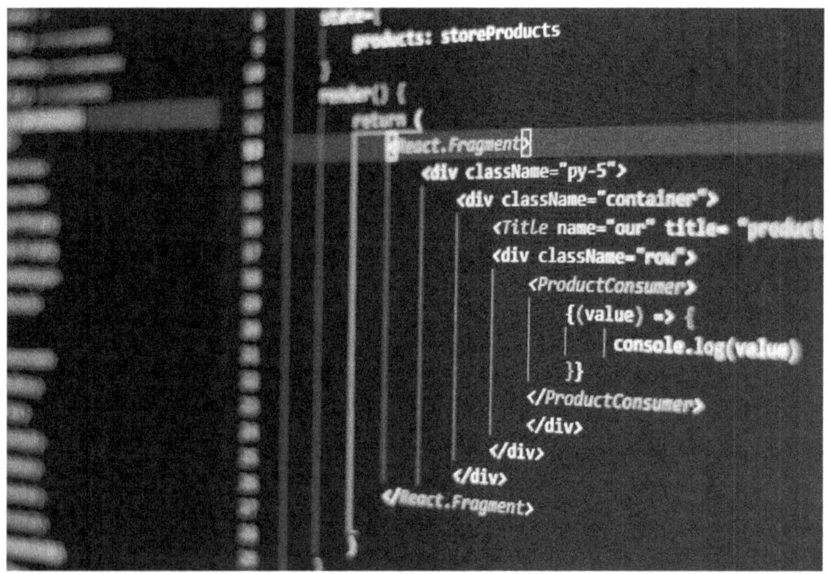

Every computer program, whether simple or complex, comprises algorithms. Algorithms are used to set up the instructions that tell a computer what to do with data and how to process it. They're also used in other ways, like designing new applications and solving mathematical problems. In this article, we'll look at algorithms and why they're so important. We'll also look at how you can use them to make your programs more efficient and effective!

Algorithms Are the Heart and Soul of Computing

Algorithms are the heart and soul of computing. They're used in every aspect of computing. Algorithms perform tasks (like sorting data), solve problems (like finding the shortest route between two points), and create solutions (like making a shopping list).

The Speed and Efficiency of a Computer Program Depend on the Algorithm

You've heard of algorithms before but don't know what they are? An algorithm is a set of rules used to solve or break down complex problems into smaller parts. For example, let's say you have a big problem: You need to make some spaghetti for your family. How do you begin? First, you could break it down into smaller parts; instead of making all the pasta yourself, maybe someone else in the house can help! Then maybe another person can grate some cheese or cut up vegetables—and so on until everyone has contributed something useful toward making dinner happen!

The point here is that breaking large problems into smaller ones allows us humans (or computers) to work more efficiently towards solving them because we're not trying to tackle everything at once. The same idea applies to algorithms: They are designed in such a way as to allow computers (or humans) to process information quicker and more effectively than if each step had been completed separately from one another.

A Very Important Aspect of Algorithms Is Their Design

A very important aspect of algorithms is their design. Algorithms can be designed to be efficient, or they can be designed to be easy to understand. Designing an algorithm is an art form that involves many considerations: how fast the program runs, how much memory it uses, and how easy it would be to debug or modify once finished.

Some algorithms have many different features (for example, sorting algorithms), while others are more specialized (such as graph traversal). You also need to consider what kind of data you want your algorithm to work with. For example, if you want your program to sort numbers, you might use a specific sorting algorithm like merge sort, which will only work on certain data types, such as integers from 0-99.

An Algorithm Should Be the Most Effective Among Many Approaches to Solving a Problem

In addition, a good algorithm should be efficient and fast, accurate in its predictions, reliable in that it will yield the same results each time it is applied, and secure from outside tampering.

Some Problems Have No Algorithms at All

Some problems have no algorithms because they are ill-defined or too hard to solve. An example of this is the problem of deciding whether a given digital circuit does or does not have an error. This problem is well-posed but has no known solution.

Another example is the Travelling Salesman Problem (TSP). The TSP asks for the shortest possible route that visits each city exactly once, and it has been proven to be NP-hard to approximate within 1% accuracy.

Algorithms Are Not Just for Computers But for Everything That Needs to Be Done in a Set of Steps

Now that we've laid down the basics of algorithms let's explore how they impact our daily lives.

Algorithms are used in all aspects of life, from working out at the gym to cooking dinner. They are the rules that govern how computers and humans work; they're even what makes animals function! If you've ever played Angry Birds or Candy Crush Saga, you know firsthand just how important algorithms are in everyday life.

Algorithms are the heart and soul of computing. They are not just for computers, but for everything that needs to be done in a set of steps. The speed and efficiency of a computer program depend on the algorithm. An algorithm should be the most effective among many approaches to solving a problem. Some problems have no algorithms at all.

Algorithms as a Technology

Algorithms are a tool that is often misunderstood and even more often abused. Algorithms are a set of rules and not just "math" (though a great deal of math is involved). Algorithms can be used to solve problems or to implement known solutions. Algorithms can be written in any language but often must be optimized, curating a solution for the programmer to their problem. Algorithms come in all shapes and sizes and can be used to solve billions of different problems. Unfortunately, not all algorithms work well in every situation and must be optimized accordingly.

Algorithms Are a Tool That Is Often Misunderstood and Even More Often Abused

They're not magic, and they don't solve all problems. Moreover, algorithms can be abused in ways that cause real harm to people. But that doesn't mean algorithms are bad; we must use them responsibly.

Algorithms are rules or instructions that tell a computer what to do. They exist in many forms, from simple recipes for baking cookies to complex mathematical equations used by physicists.

Algorithms are everywhere, and they're not going away. They're getting more complicated and ubiquitous by the day. If you use a search engine or social media platform, you encounter an algorithm every time you log in. You can also find them in many other places: from self-driving cars to smart home devices like Alexa and Google Home.

The algorithms that power our digital lives are complex and often proprietary. That means we don't know exactly what they do or how they work. But it also means that they could be used to manipulate us in ways we can't even imagine. For example, algorithms are increasingly being used to make decisions about people's lives—like whether someone gets a job or their parole is granted. And when humans aren't involved in making these decisions, it can lead to mistakes (or worse).

Algorithms Are a Set of Rules and Not Just "Math"

When people talk about algorithms, they usually think of math. While algorithms are often used in math and computer science, they're not just math. Algorithms are rules that tell you how to solve a problem with a computer. The rules can be simple or complex, but they all do the same: take input data and return an answer based on how the rule works.

Some algorithms are very easy to understand because their rules are simple. For example, if you want to know what number comes after 5, then all you have to do is add 1! However, other algorithms are more complicated because their rules involve multiple steps and variables that change over time as we move through our code execution path. So, in this example, if we want to find out which number comes after 5, we would need a counter of some description.

Algorithms Can Be Used to Solve Problems or to Implement Known Solutions

Algorithms can be used to solve problems or to implement known solutions. When you are using an algorithm to solve a problem, you are breaking the problem down into smaller chunks and solving them one at a time. For example, if you wanted to find the square root of a number that is not an integer, you could use the following algorithm:

- Define your variables: x = number; y = result;

- Setup initial conditions: $z = x - 1$; $r = 0$; $t = 2 + zk-1 - xk-1$ (where k is an integer)

- Start looping until num_iterations == 0 (or some other condition): while num_iterations > 0 do /* repeated steps below */ `endwhile`

- Calculate y := computesquare(x);

- Return y as the answer

Algorithms Can Be Written in Any Language, But Often Must Be Optimized, Curating a Solution for the Programmer to Their Problem

Algorithms aren't just math. They're a set of rules that can be written in any language. They are optimized but often must be optimized for the programmer's problem.

Algorithms Come in All Shapes and Sizes and Can Be Used to Solve Billions of Different Problems

As a technology, algorithms come in all shapes and sizes and can be used to solve billions of different problems. But what is an algorithm? What does it mean?

In short, an algorithm is a set of rules that guide you toward solving a problem or implementing known solutions. It's not just math; it's also logic. For example, if you want to find someone on social media who has a specific interest in something (say cats. Then the way you get to that person is by following certain steps:

- Looking at their profile page

- Searching for keywords related to your interests (like "cat")

- Filtering results according to their location or age range

All these steps are part of one big algorithm. This process might seem simple at first glance, but when we start breaking down each step into smaller ones, we can quickly see how complex algorithms are!

Not All Algorithms Work Well in Every Situation and Must Be Optimized Accordingly

Not all algorithms are created equal. For example, one algorithm might work well when the data set has a small number of variables but be completely unsuited to an exponentially larger sample size. For example:

A common algorithm in machine learning is linear regression, which finds the best fit line between two variables based on their historical relationship (the slope and intercept). The more data points you have, the better this algorithm works because it gives you more information to make predictions. However, if your data has many variables (hundreds or thousands), this algorithm becomes less useful because there are too many parameters to consider at once. So instead of finding the best fit line between hundreds or thousands of variables at once—which would be impossible. Instead, you can use an alternative machine-learning algorithm like K-means clustering that distributes your points into clusters based on their distances from each other first before fitting them into lines later.

A Well-Implemented Algorithm Can Save Tremendous Amounts of Time Compared to Manual Labor

An algorithm is a set of rules and operations used to solve problems or implement known solutions. It can be used in many different ways and written in any language. The most famous algorithms have been around for decades and have seen countless revisions, optimizations, and improvements as we learn more about them.

Algorithms are often categorized by their uses: an algorithm may be used to find something (like the shortest path between two locations) or simply store information (like the phone number of your favorite restaurant). In this case, we're talking about algorithms designed to take data from one set state and transform it into another. Using a series of steps that either transform each item individually or produce results from those items' interactions, all without introducing error into whichever part of reality it's designed for!

Understanding Algorithms' Intricacies Can Help Develop a Better Perspective on the Current Technology Landscape

Algorithms can be used to solve problems or implement known solutions. When a programmer is trying to find a solution for their problem, they may first use other algorithms and processes to derive the final algorithm from them. The final algorithm should be optimized to run efficiently with as few resources as possible. This can be done by either changing things like memory usage or time complexity or optimizing the code's overall structure.

Algorithms can be written in any language but often must be optimized and curated to work within certain hardware constraints (for example, an embedded system may have less memory than your laptop). This can mean making alterations, such as removing unnecessary data structures or improving loops so that each iteration uses fewer resources.

Chapter 2

Getting Started

Insertion Sort

Insertion sort is the simplest sorting algorithm. It is a linear time algorithm and uses only one pass over the data set. Insertion sort works by comparing adjacent elements, swapping them if needed, and then inserting all elements in the correct order before comparing the next pair of adjacent elements in the list.

The Concept behind Insertion Sort

The concept behind insertion sort is simple: we want to sort an array of items in ascending order by inserting them into their correct positions in the array.

We start by placing the first item in the sorted array at the beginning of the array. Then, we go through it and insert every other item into its correct place as long as it doesn't cause a change in comparison with any other element already placed.

Time Complexity of Insertion Sort

Insertion sort has a time complexity of O(n2), meaning it takes as much time to sort n elements as it would sort n2 elements. So, for example, if you have 50 elements to sort and your computer can do 1 billion operations per second (a pretty fast computer), it will take 100,000 seconds (which is about 17 hours) to finish the job.

While insertion sort is slow for large data sets, it's great for small ones—it can easily be faster than other algorithms when sorting thousands of numbers or strings!

Advantages of Insertion Sort

Insertion sort is a simple sorting algorithm implemented in a few lines of code. It is often used for small data sets because it does not require much memory and can be implemented quickly.

It's also stable, which means that if you sort an array of integers with insertion sort, the original order of equal values will remain unchanged after the sort is complete. This makes insertion sort useful for sorting arrays of numbers where you need to keep track of their relative positions. For example, if you have an array representing a deck of cards and want to know their order after they've been shuffled together into one big stack (a process called "shuffling").

Disadvantages of Insertion Sort

Insertion sort has a high constant time cost. Therefore, insertion sort is not suitable for large data sets. In addition, insertion sort is not suitable for unsorted data.

Insertion sort is not suitable for sorted data or partially sorted data.

When to Use Insertion Sort

- If you have a small data set and want to sort it quickly, insertion sort is great.

- If the data set is already sorted, insertion sort can be used to sort it even more quickly. (It's not quite as fast as merge sort or quicksort for already-sorted data sets, but still pretty good.)

- If the data set is already partially sorted, insertion sort will take care of the rest!

Insertion Sort Is Used for Small Data Sets Due to Its Low Time Complexity Compared to Other Algorithms

Insertion sort is a basic sorting algorithm that uses a simple but efficient method to sort data. Insertion sort was created in 1945 by John von Neumann and published in his paper "Theory of Self-Reproducing Automata." Unfortunately, this algorithm was invented before other sorting algorithms (such as heapsort or merge sort) were developed and has had little improvement since then.

Because insertion sort works slowly with large amounts of data and poorly performs when duplicates are in the list, it is not often used for large arrays. However, for small lists (especially those already sorted), insertion sort runs very quickly without causing much overhead during its execution.

This algorithm is used to sort an array of integers with the restriction that its length is less than or equal to 10. The algorithm uses two arrays: one holds the original unsorted array, and another holds a sorted copy (called "temp"). This algorithm is simple and can be implemented in any programming language. However, since insertion sort has a worst-case time complexity of $O(n^2)$, it should not be used if you need to sort large arrays whose length exceeds 10 items.

Analyzing Algorithms

Algorithms are the building blocks of computer science. They can be simple and elegant or complex and intricate, but regardless of how they look on the surface, they always have some structure that makes them work as intended. Moreover, this structure can make them easier to understand than you might think: we just need to break down their pieces into smaller parts and look at them more closely. The best way to do this is by using a technique called "analysis," which involves breaking an algorithm apart so that we can understand its behavior step by step.

How Fast Does the Algorithm Grow?

The growth of an algorithm is the number of operations it performs as a function of its input size. For example, if you have a binary search algorithm and it takes 1 operation to compare two items, then the growth rate is 2 (since there are two comparisons per item).

In general, we would like algorithms that have polynomial time complexity — this means that the running time of an algorithm grows at most, like some constant times n (where n is the number of elements in your input). Unfortunately, if you double your input size, your running time only increases by a constant amount. Exponential growth can be bad because it means as soon as you get past some small input size threshold, like 10 or 100 inputs. So even though you've doubled your workload by increasing from 1M elements to 2M elements, your program still takes 50x longer than when there were only 1 million elements instead!

Are There Any Obvious Bottlenecks?

The first step to fixing a bottleneck is identifying it. You can use the following two questions to identify a bottleneck:

- Are there any obvious bottlenecks?

- What's the cost of running the algorithm?

An obvious bottleneck is usually caused by input data or some part of the algorithm. For example, suppose you've written an algorithm that inputs a large amount of data and processes it sequentially. for example, it reads one row from a database table at a time. In that case, you may run into performance issues if your machine has limited memory capacity or its disk accessing speed is too slow.

Is There a Related Problem That Might Be Easier to Solve?

You can look at the same problem but break it into smaller pieces. For example, if you were trying to find the shortest route between two cities in a graph, you could instead work on finding the distance from A to B by looking at city pairs adjacent to each other (the neighbors of A). This is an easier problem because it doesn't require information about all possible pairs of cities.

Another way this concept is used is when there isn't enough data for your algorithm to be useful. For example, if you have 100 people you want to predict whether they will vote for your candidate or not, only 20% of them have made their choice public. Then even though most algorithms would consider 80% of people "unknown," this means nothing—you don't have enough information! In these cases where there isn't enough data, we often use heuristics or random sampling rather than more complex methods (though sometimes both approaches may be necessary).

What Are the Important Parts of the Input Data?

The input data is the information you use to solve a problem. These pieces of information can vary in size, complexity, and even whether they are real-world or artificial.

Sometimes you might have a huge dataset with many columns and rows, but it's just not going to be useful for solving your problem. Instead, you'll want to reduce this large dataset into something smaller and more manageable so that it's easier for your algorithm to process. However, if your problem requires you to use all of these columns and rows, then there's no need for simplification!

You may also have a small number of columns or rows in an input dataset, but you still find yourself running into issues when trying different algorithms. This is because some algorithms work better with larger numbers (they're called scalable) while others work better with smaller ones (non-scalable). So, ask yourself: "Is my model scalable?"

Can I Generate Similar Input Data That Is Not Quite Big But Still Big Enough to Exhibit the Same Behavior?

Suppose you have a large dataset and want to ensure that your algorithm works properly. In that case, ensuring that the data you're using represents what you'd expect in the real world is important. If you have the capacity, you can generate a smaller data set with similar characteristics as your large dataset. You can then evaluate how well your algorithm performs on this smaller data set and compare it with how well it performs on your original large dataset.

If these results are different for any reason (for example, if one method was faster on one but slower on the other), it gives some insight into where improvements may be needed in efficiency or effectiveness.

Can I Think of Some Easy-to-State Properties of the Solution That Are True When the Answer Is Correct?

Consider the following question: What is the value of x in the following equation?

```
x = (3 * y) + 2
```

The answer is 11. However, it might not be immediately obvious how to come up with this answer. You might want to try different values for x until you find one that works or start plugging in numbers at random until you get an answer that seems plausible. But there's another way: you can use mathematics to solve problems like these! One thing we know about this problem is that x must be some multiple of 2 and 3; so, let's see what happens when we multiply both sides by 2 and 3, respectively:

```
formula_1\frac{2}{11} = \frac{9}{11}
=>\frac{1}{11} = \frac{3}{5}\endash
```

A little more thinking will reveal that no matter what number I choose for x, I will always get 5/11 as my result! This means we've found our property: it's true when our answer is correct; not true when our answer isn't correct!

Can I Find a Solution By Reusing Parts of Previous Solutions to Slightly Smaller Instances of the Problem?

You can use dynamic programming to solve a problem by breaking it into subproblems and solving each subproblem repeatedly. For example, if you are working with a recurrence relation, the solution will be obtained by saving the results of previous subproblems as needed. Dynamic programming is also known as memorization or table lookups.

You Can Do Many Things to Examine Your Algorithm More Closely

When analyzing algorithms, you can do many things to examine your algorithm more closely.

- How fast does the algorithm grow? Using an algorithm that grows too fast is generally not a good idea.

- Are there any obvious bottlenecks? If so, try removing or changing them so they don't slow down the rest of your program as much.

- Is there a related problem that might be easier to solve? For example, if you're looking at how long it takes two people to compare their folders of files, but one person has very few files. In contrast, if another person has many files, then maybe instead, you should focus on comparing two random files from each folder rather than comparing all pairs of files from both folders (where each pair would involve two distinct files from each folder).

Chapter 3

Recurrences and Function Growth

The Recurrences Substitution Method

A substitution method is a common tool that can be used to solve recurrences. It is often easy to use and requires little to no guessing or creativity, making it the ideal solution for simple problems. Let's look at an example of how the substitution method works and its strengths and limitations.

The Substitution Method Is Commonly Used to Solve Recurrences, As It Is Often Easy to Use and Requires Little to No Guessing or Creativity

The substitution method is fairly commonly used to solve recurrences, as it is often easy to use and requires little to no guessing or creativity.

The substitution method involves finding an expression of the function that can be substituted into the original problem, which leads us straight to its solution.

- $f(n) = 2f(n-1) + 2n + 1$

- $g(n) = f(n)+1$

Let's Take a Look at an Example of the Substitution Method

Let's take a look at an example of the substitution method. In this case, we'll solve the recurrence:

- If n is even, then n/2 is an integer.

- If n is odd and greater than 1, then n/2 + 1 is an integer (and so on).

Now let's assume that this recurrence holds. We'll start by assuming that n = 4 and seeing what happens:

```
* 4/2 = 2 * 2 + 1 = 3 * 3 + 1 = 7
```

Since we know that 4 was even greater than 1, we see that 7 must be an integer too! So far, so good! Let's try one more value for n:

```
5/2 = 2.5 * 2 + 1 = 5 * 3 + 1 = 11 * 11/2 =
5.5 * 5.5 + 1 = 20
```

This time, we see that 20 is not an integer! Since we know that 5 was odd and greater than 1, this result is not a contradiction of our assumption that the recurrence holds for all values of n. Therefore, it must be true!

A Common Application of the Substitution Method Is to Recurrences That Are Expensive to Compute

The substitution method is a good tool to use when you have a difficult recurrence to solve. It doesn't provide a silver-bullet solution, but it does help us by making the problem easier to deal with. Here's an example:

Let's say we want to compute the following sequence:

```
$S_n = \begin{cases} 1 & \text{if } n \leq 0
\\ 3n + 1 & \text{if } n > 0.\end{cases}$
```

We can use substitution to find S_{10} instead of doing all those multiplications individually.

We make an assumption: Let's assume that if we replace each instance of n in our recurrence with some other constant (like one or zero), then what remains will also be a valid statement about our original sequence S_n. In other words, if we replace every occurrence of n with some other constant and simplify everything down as much as possible, then the result should still be true for all cases except where there was previously an occurrence of a.

The Substitution Method Is Not a Silver-Bullet Solution to Recurrences; There Are Cases Where It May Fail

First, it can be difficult to find the right factorization of a particular expression (using the substitution method). So, if you're trying to solve a recurrence but can't think of how to factorize it using repeated substitution, don't worry! There are other methods out there that help with this part. For example, one method involves using induction on an increasing sequence of terms in an expression until you get down to basic arithmetic operations (like multiplication and addition), which reduce down easily into simple cases like power towers or factorials, respectively.

Second, the substitution technique only works for a certain class of problems called linear recurrences, which require calculating successive values from previous ones using only addition or multiplication operations (i.e., no exponents). Unfortunately, this means that many important types of recurrence—such as those involving polynomials—are outside its scope because they involve more complicated operations such as exponentiation and logarithms, as well as addition/multiplication alone! The good news, however, is that many other methods are available now which solve these types too!

With Practice, You'll Be Able to Leverage the Substitution Method to Your Advantage!

There are a lot of reasons to practice. If you're preparing for a big exam, it will help you feel more comfortable and confident when the time comes. If you're working on your basketball dribbling skills, practicing will help train your muscles in the best way possible. And if you're trying to learn how to do something new like this method, then practice is crucial!

The best way to start practicing is by finding an exercise similar but easier than you want to master. For example, if I'm learning how to juggle three balls with my right hand, I can first try juggling two balls with both hands instead—that's still challenging, but less so than three balls would be at first glance because fewer things are happening at once (2 vs. 3). Then once I'm comfortable with two balls in each hand, I could start adding another ball or two until, eventually, I can juggle all three as smoothly as possible without dropping them too often.

Growth of Functions

Algorithms are a set of rules or guidelines used to solve a problem. It is usually a series of steps that must be performed to obtain the desired result. The word "algorithm" comes from Arabic, meaning "the art of calculating." In mathematics and computer science, algorithms are specific instructions for calculating mathematical functions.

Asymptotic Notation

Asymptotic notation describes how algorithms perform as the size of the problem grows.

There are two types: big-O and little-o. Big-O notation describes worst-case behavior, while little o describes average case behavior. However, both are useful in understanding what an algorithm will do in practice, independent of its implementation details or any particular inputs to consider.

Big O notation is usually written using Greek letters, like Omega or Theta. It's a way of describing an algorithm's performance over time, no matter what kind of input you give (so long as it's not infinite). For example, if you're trying out an algorithm for yourself and your program starts running slower and slower with bigger numbers on its input range (i), then you can use this notation to describe your findings by saying that "this function has growth rate $O(n)$."

Big O Notation

Big O notation is a concept that is used to compare the rate of growth of an algorithm. It can predict how long an algorithm will take, even if you don't know any other details about it, such as the size of its input. Big O notation is based on the idea that most functions can be described by one or more constants and variables, allowing us to compare different functions by looking at them.

Big O notation can also be used when comparing algorithms: If you know that $f(n)$ grows faster than $g(n)$, then any result you get from running f will probably finish faster than if you ran g. Because big O notation allows us to compare how quickly a function grows without knowing anything about its input or output values, we can use it as an approximation for many problems involving finding efficient solutions for all math problems.

Theta Notation

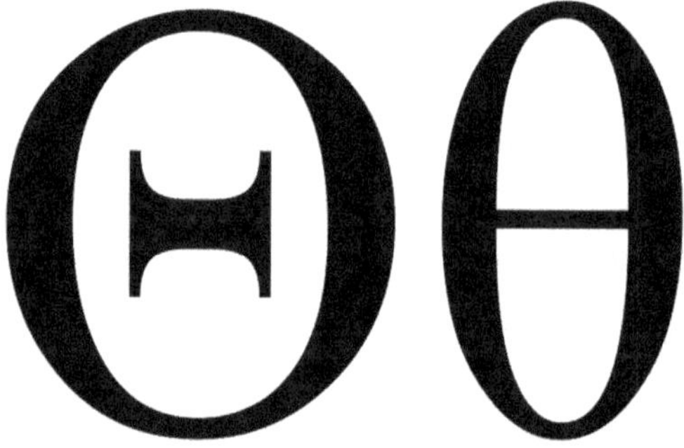

Theta notation is a way to describe the growth of functions when their inputs are large and small. Theta notation uses symbols to represent the function's value at any time, where t represents time, x represents the input, and θ(t) represents output.

The equation for the change in function value over one unit of time is given by:

```
Δf = f(x + 1) - f(x), where Δ = change and f
= function.
```

Omega Notation

Theta (Θ) is the lower bound of the function, and Omega (Ω) is the upper bound. Alpha (α) is the value of a function at a given point.

```
Alpha(x)= f(x)*e^(-delta*x/h), where:

f(x)= value of function at x

delta = step size for iteration

h = number of iterations
```

Designing Algorithms

A good algorithm is the backbone of any useful application. It's a set of instructions that can be used to solve problems. Algorithms are like recipes: they'll tell you exactly what steps to take and which ingredients to use, but they won't cook dinner for you. You need something else—a computer or some other processor—to execute the instructions in an algorithm.

Use Data Structures to Organize Your Data, So They Are Useful

Data structures are the way you organize your data. They're made up of data and the operations that can be performed on them, making it easy to perform common operations.

Data structures help you solve problems because they make it possible to do things like keep track of how many people are in a building or how long it takes to get from one place to another.

You can use different data structures depending on what kind of problem you're trying to solve, which makes designing algorithms fun!

Use the Right Data Structure for the Job

When designing an algorithm, you must consider the data structure(s) used. Different data structures support different operations, and some are better suited for some structures than others. For example, if you want to look up a specific item in a collection or insert an item into a collection, you should use a dictionary. On the other hand, if you need to find items that share some property (e.g., all vegetables), then it makes sense to use sets instead.

Consider this example of trying to find a number between 1 and 100:

```python
def find_number_in_range():
numbers = []
```

```
for i in range(1, 101): if i % 2 == 0:"`
```

This code works fine but is inefficient because it uses two loops: one over all integers between 1 and 100 and the other overall odd integers between 1 and 100. This is bad because Python compiles small loops into machine code which runs very fast on modern processors; wasting cycles by doing extra work can lead to slower execution times overall!

Keep Algorithms Simple and Clean

The first step in designing an algorithm is to keep it simple and clean. Make sure your code doesn't add unnecessary complexity or take more time than necessary to complete. If parts of the algorithm don't need to be there, don't be afraid to throw them away or simplify them as much as possible. Over-engineering a solution can lead to unnecessarily large code and make it difficult for others (and you!) to work with after the fact.

Keep Only What You Need

Designing algorithms is all about keeping only what you need. This means you should only keep what you need to solve the problem. If something is not used in the solution, don't keep it! Throw it away if possible; otherwise, put it aside until later when there might be a time when it can be useful (in other words, write down any information that may become useful for reuse).

Throw Away What You Don't Need

It's tempting to keep everything, but your goal is to have the smallest codebase possible that works. The best way to do this is by identifying what exactly doesn't work anymore and then getting rid of it.

If there are pieces of code or data that don't seem relevant anymore (or haven't been used in a while), consider cutting them out entirely. If they're still required for other parts of the algorithm, then those parts should be refactored to use only existing components instead of introducing new ones; if nothing depends on them anymore, remove them!

Find Opportunities to Reuse Parts of Algorithms

Reusing code saves time and effort, as well as potential space. If you have a function that does what you need it to do, use that same function again!

The benefits of finding ways to reuse code are:

- You save time because your program doesn't have to repeat work (and thus, you can get the job done faster)

- You save space because your programs won't be so large (which may be important if they're running on resource-limited devices)

- You save effort because there's less work for you or others who maintain the code in the future (if someone else needs to change something about an algorithm, later on, it'll take them less time)

Leave Room for Optimization

When you design an algorithm, it's important to leave room for optimization. The common case should be optimized first; later, when the algorithm has been implemented, you can go back and optimize for exceptional cases. You may also decide that optimization is unnecessary or would be too difficult to implement in your programming language of choice.

In addition to being a good idea from a performance standpoint, optimizing for the common case has another benefit: simplicity! For example, suppose you optimize for every possible case before implementing your algorithms. In that case, your code will take longer to write and will be less legible than if you focused on the common cases and left room for further optimization later.

Chapter 4

Randomized Algorithms and Probabilistic Analysis

Randomized Algorithms

Randomized algorithms are a type of algorithm that uses randomization to solve problems. This is different from deterministic algorithms, which always give the same answer every time they are run on the same input data. The advantage of using a randomized algorithm is that, for some problems, it can be more efficient than deterministic methods. For example, if you want to sort a list of numbers in descending order but don't know how many numbers there will be (for example, your system might receive any number between 1 and 10 million). Then it would be faster to just choose each number randomly from the list and compare them one by one until you find out which one should go first. In this case, there is no way to do this without randomization!

What Is the Advantage of Using a Randomized Algorithm?

There are a few benefits to using a randomized algorithm:

- It can solve problems that would otherwise require too much time.

- It can solve problems that would otherwise require too much memory.

- It can solve problems requiring too much space on discs or other media (e.g., hard drives).

- If you only have access to processors with limited capabilities (e.g., an embedded system), a randomized algorithm may be your best option for solving certain problems efficiently and reliably.

What Are Some of the Different Types of Randomized Algorithms?

You can find several different randomized algorithms. Here are a few:

- **Monte Carlo** is used to solve problems in which the probability distribution of the solution is known, but its exact value is not. This algorithm uses random sampling to approximate solutions to problems by repeated random sampling from the solution space and then averaging over many samples. An example of this might be finding an optimal placement for a new building on the land, so it doesn't interfere with any other buildings. There are many possible locations for each building, and interference between them can have very complex effects on their functions. For example, if one building blocks out light from another. In this case, we know that by choosing an appropriate set of locations for all our buildings, we will have a good solution; however, we don't know what those locations are ahead of time because there are too many possibilities! So instead, we choose a subset at random and average over all possible subsets until we get close enough to our goal solution (in other words: by averaging over many samples).

- **Simulated Annealing** solves optimization problems using simulated "natural" processes such as temperature fluctuations or physical diffusion through matter, allowing it to search large spaces efficiently while maintaining high-quality results.

- **Markov Chain Monte Carlo (MCMC)** is similar but uses stochastic simulation methods rather than thermodynamics simulations to achieve better performance.

- **Randomized Quicksort** selects elements at each step based on chance rather than location; this allows us to apply quick selection repeatedly without worrying about how much data has been sorted already so long as everything after that point remains unordered.

When Should You Not Use a Randomized Algorithm?

There are a few instances in which a randomized algorithm might not be the best choice for your problem.

- If you need to know how long the algorithm will take to run—for example, if you have a deadline for when an answer is needed—you will have to use another type of algorithm instead.

- If you need to be able to predict the outcome of an algorithm, again, use one that isn't random (the most common kind of nonrandomized algorithm is deterministic).

- And finally, if you have a lot of data and need to process it efficiently, then using a randomized algorithm would likely be too slow.

Sometimes, Using a Randomized Algorithm Is Better Than a Deterministic One

Sometimes, using a randomized algorithm is better than a deterministic one. In this section, we'll cover randomized algorithms' advantages and disadvantages.

In theory, there's no reason why you can't use any kind of algorithm for any problem. However, in practice, there are many cases where a randomized algorithm is better than a deterministic one. This happens for two reasons:

- You have limited time to get your result (or else you're willing to wait several days)

- The problem you're trying to solve has too many variables or parameters (this might happen if your task involves a lot of people working together)

Probabilistic Analysis

Probabilistic analysis is a field of mathematics that uses probability theory as a tool to make statements about events in the real world. The subject can be divided into two parts:

- **Probability Theory** deals with events that are capable of being observed (and thus have some sort of likelihood), and

- **Probability Models** deal with events that cannot be observed directly but can be modeled using probabilities. This module will focus on probability models.

Probabilistic Analysis is the study of random phenomena. Mathematicians developed the field of probability in the 17th century. The first person to use the word "probability" was Gerolamo Cardano in 1613. He defined it as: "the art of assigning to an event a number expressing how likely it is." In other words, if a coin has two sides and each side is equally likely or probable, then when you flip this coin, there's one out of two (or 50%) chances for getting heads and one out of two chances for getting tails.

The term "probability theory" stems from Laplace's work on astronomy. He showed that all physical processes could be reduced into mathematical equations that are inherently probabilistic, so much so that we can make statements about them based on our knowledge about their behavior! For example: suppose someone asks us whether today's weather is more like Tuesday or Wednesday. Of course, we could consult weather forecasts before deciding which day our answer should favor, but these predictions are notoriously inaccurate! So instead, let's use our knowledge gained through experience with past Tuesdays/Wednesdays/Thursdays, etc. Then, looking at what happened previously under similar circumstances (elements such as temperature), we can confidently say that today will probably feel similar because those conditions were similar too."

Two Types of Probability

There are two types of probability:

- **Theoretical probability** is the ratio of favorable outcomes over all possible outcomes. For example, if you're rolling a single die and want to know the theoretical probability of getting a 1 (1/6), you would divide 1 by 6, or 0.16666.

- **Empirical or relative frequency probability** occurs when testing an experiment many times. If you rolled a die 100 times and got 30 ones in that period, then your empirical or relative frequency would be 0.3 (30/100).

A Language for Expressing Uncertainty

Probability is a language for expressing uncertainty. It is a way to express the degree of belief in an event, especially if the event cannot be observed directly and if its outcome can take on two or more values. In other words, if you don't exactly know what will happen, but you are pretty sure it won't be one thing or another (and maybe there's some probability it could be both). Then using probabilities is a way to communicate that information.

Probabilities are often shorthand when communicating uncertain events; for example:

"What are your chances of getting this disease given your lifestyle?"

"I think there's a 60% chance we'll get pregnant this month."

"The odds of winning this game are 3:1 against; that means if you bet $10,000 on it, you will only win $30,000 if you win."

Probabilistic Modeling

Probabilistic models are used to describe the uncertainty of a system. They are most often used in the field of machine learning, where they help computers make decisions based on available data without being able to know everything about a situation. A probabilistic model can be represented as a graph representing an event with branches representing possible outcomes and probabilities of each outcome occurring (or not). For example, let's say you want to know if it's likely that you'll get a raise at work next year. Using this type of model, you could create one branch for "yes," which has an 80% probability; another branch for "no," with 20% probability; and various other branches for any other possibilities (such as getting fired or quitting).

Examples of Probabilistic Models

Probabilistic models are used in many fields, including:

- Computer science

- Game theory

- Machine learning

- Operations research (management science)

- Probability theory and statistics

Calculus of Variations, Convexity, and Duality Theory

The calculus of variations, a generalization of probability and statistics, is a method for solving optimization problems. This method attempts to find a function's maximum or minimum value by assuming that it is not attainable and then determining whether or not other functions achieve this same result. The difference between these two values can be calculated as an error measure or loss function. This process can be repeated many times with different random variables until you find one that has a minimal error when compared to your original function (called duality theory).

The dual of any given function is another function that produces exactly opposite results; for example, if one function increases in value over time, then its dual decreases in value over time at the same rate.

Applications

Probability theory has applications in many sciences, engineering, and mathematics fields. Some areas where probability and statistics are fundamental include:

- Statistics

- Financial Mathematics

- Econometrics

- Systems and control theory Mathematical biology

- Biological pattern recognition Chemical engineering

Duality Can Be Considered to Be a Generalization of Probability/Statistics

Duality is a generalization of probability theory and statistics. It has many applications in physics, engineering, and finance.

Duality is a powerful tool for solving problems. For example, many physical phenomena are governed by laws that depend on the values of certain variables; these variables are known as the "control parameters" or "forcing functions." In many cases, we can choose values for these variables that limit our problem to a simpler one with fewer degrees of freedom (i.e., fewer degrees of freedom per equation). This approach is known as "dual representation.

Duality is a very powerful tool in mathematics, and we have only scratched the surface of its applications here. You must understand that duality can be used to describe nonlinear and linear functions—and sometimes even both at once!

Chapter 5

Quicksort

Quicksort is a sorting algorithm that takes an array of unsorted data and returns a sorted collection.

Quicksort is an in-place sorting algorithm that doesn't require additional memory to store the result. It also doesn't use any more memory than necessary because only the elements being swapped are moved around; other elements remain in their original positions after each invocation of the recursive function.

Quicksort is a recursive algorithm, meaning it calls itself repeatedly until there are no more iterations remaining for which further recursion makes sense or some terminating condition has been met. Recursion allows us to tackle larger problems by breaking them down into smaller parts that can be solved independently before combining them later on--like breaking up a problem into multiple subgoals and working on those before tackling anything else!

Finally, quicksort may not be efficient at all if your dataset isn't already sorted (or nearly so). But, again, this depends on specifics such as the array size and what you're trying to accomplish with quicksort.

Partitioning

To sort an array, Quicksort uses a partitioning algorithm to split the array into two parts: one with elements less than the pivot and one with elements greater than the pivot. The basic idea is that each time it's called on an element in the array, if it finds that its value (if less than or equal to pivot) or its index (if greater than pivot) belongs in one of the two sub-arrays, then it swaps their positions. Finally, after this has been done enough until there are no more moves left to make, you have your sorted array!

Quicksort Algorithm

- Quicksort is a randomized algorithm, which means that the order in which elements are sorted will change each time you run it.

- Quicksort is a divide-and-conquer algorithm that divides an array into two parts and recursively sorts them (see step 5). This way, quicksort will run in linear time if your array has less than half its elements left to sort after partitioning. If your array has more than half of its elements left to sort after partitioning, quicksort will run in quadratic time and will be slower than other algorithms, like merge sort or heapsort, that only require one pass over the whole input array.

So, how do you use it? The first step is to sort an array.

The second step is to recur on smaller subarrays until you reach one that can be sorted in place.

The third step is to recur on smaller subarrays until they, too, can be sorted in place or until there are no more subarrays (and the entire array has been sorted).

Quicksort Is a Divide and Conquer Algorithm

Quicksort is a divide and conquer algorithm, which means that it consists of two main steps:

- **Divide step** – Partition the array into two parts: one with elements less than or equal to the pivot element and one with elements greater than the pivot element.

- **Conquer step** – Sort each subarray recursively using quicksort, then combine them back into a sorted array.

This algorithm is extremely efficient and can be used as a sorting technique. As a result, Quicksort has many applications in computer science and data structures.

Randomized Quicksort Algorithm

Randomized Quicksort is a sorting algorithm that works by partitioning an array into two parts and then recursively sorting the two partitions. The main advantage of using a randomized version of quicksort is that it is guaranteed to run in $O(n \log n)$ time, even in the worst case. The disadvantage is that it is slightly more complex to implement than the traditional quicksort algorithm.

How the Algorithm Works

The randomized quicksort algorithm works by first selecting a pivot element from the array. The pivot element can be chosen in many ways, but a common method is selecting the element randomly. Once the pivot element has been selected, all other elements in the array are partitioned into groups: those that are less than or equal to the pivot element and those greater than the pivot element.

The randomized quicksort algorithm then recursively sorts each of the two partitions. In other words, it sorts the subarray of elements that are less than or equal to the pivot element and the subarray of elements greater than the pivot element. Once both partitions have been sorted, the entire array will be sorted.

There are a few different ways to implement randomized quicksort, but one of the most common methods is known as Hoare's partitioning scheme. This method works by selecting a pivot element and then rearranging the elements in the array so that all elements that are less than or equal to the pivot element come before it. All elements that are greater than the pivot element come after it.

The code for Hoare's partitioning scheme is as follows:

```
def randomized quicksort (A, left,
right):

    if left < right:

        q = hoare_partition (A, left,
right)
```

```
        randomized quicksort (A, left, q
-1)

        randomized quicksort (A Ly +1,
right)

    def hoare_partition (A, left ,right):

    x = A[right] #pivot value

    i = left - 1 #scanning pointer j
#border pointer for bigger values for j in
range (left , right ): if A[j] <= x: i += 1
exchange (A,-i ) j -= A[j] return i+1 # last
position with smaller values x = A[i ]
#pivot value exchange (A,-j ) j -= A[i ]
exchange (A,-i ) i -= 1 exchange (A,-j ) j -
= 1 return j+1 # last position with bigger
values j += [x] return i+1 # lastposition
with smaller values x = A [-j] #pivot value
exchange (A,[-i]) i += -(*A)[-j] (*A)[-j] =
x return i+1; // lastposition with smaller
values}
```

Real-Life Examples

Imagine you have a list of names you need to alphabetize: Anna, Beta, Charlie, David, and Elsa. You could sort these names by writing them out on individual index cards and then reorganizing them into alphabetical order (selection sort), or you could use a more efficient method like quicksort. Here's how quicksort would work on this particular list:

1. First, we choose a pivot element--we'll choose "David" as our pivot since he's alphabetically in the middle of our list. Then, we put all the elements before David in one pile (Anna and Beta) and all the elements after David in another (Charlie and Elsa). This leaves us with two subarrays that we can now sort independently from each other using quicksort:

    Subarray 1: Anna, Beta   Subarray 2: Charlie, Elsa

2. Next, we select a new pivot for each subarray--for Subarray 1, we'll use "Anna" since she's first alphabetically, and for Subarray 2, we'll use "Elsa" since she's last alphabetically. Now we put all the elements before our new pivots in one pile and all the elements after our new pivots in another:

Subarray 1-1:   Subarray 1-2: Beta   Subarray 2-1: Charlie
Subarray 2-2:

3. We don't have any more elements to put into piles for either subarray since our original lists only had four names (remember our base case!). This means that both of our subarrays are now sorted, so we can move on to step 4.

4. Finally, we put everything back together into one sorted list by concatenating our four sorted sub lists together--Subarray 1-1 + Subarray 1-2 + Subarray 2-1 + Subarray 2-2--which gives us our final answer:

Final answer: Anna, Beta, Charlie, David, Elsa

As our example above, quicksort is a powerful sorting algorithm that can help you quickly and efficiently put large data sets into order! However, it's important to remember that quicksort isn't right for every situation. if your data set isn't randomly distributed or you're working with a linked list instead of an array. Another sorting algorithm might be a better choice for you, like insertion sort. But if you're looking for a fast and effective way to sort an array, give quicksort a try!

Store Manager Example

The store manager has been tasked with organizing the aisles by product type. In other words, all the products in each aisle must be the same type. The products in the store are currently sorted by price from lowest to highest. The manager decides to use Quicksort to sort the products by type, making it easier for customers to find what they are looking for.

The first step is to choose a pivot element. Next, the pivot element divides the array into two smaller subarrays. The manager uses the product in the middle of the array as the pivot element.

Next, the manager needs to partition the array. Partitioning is the process of rearranging the array so that all the elements that are less than the pivot element are on one side of the pivot element, and all the elements that are greater than the pivot element are on the other side.

After partitioning, the array looks like this:

```
[2, 1, 3, 5, 4]
```

The 2 and 3 are on one side of the pivot (4) and 1 and 5 are on the other.

Now, all left is sorting each subarray recursively using Quicksort until each subarray contains only one element and is sorted.

Quicksort is a sorting algorithm that uses partitioning to divide an array into smaller subarrays. In our example, we used Quicksort to help a store manager sort products by type. First, we chose a pivot element and then partitioned our array around that element. Finally, we sorted each subarray recursively until each one only contained one element and was sorted.

Analysis of Quicksort

Quick sort is a sorting algorithm that works by selecting a "pivot" and partitioning the data around the pivot. The algorithm then recursively calls itself on smaller partitions until all elements are sorted. The efficiency of Quicksort comes from two key properties:

- **Convexity**: It is always possible to find an efficient pivot point by comparing elements with the one before or after in any given list (so long as they are not already similar). In addition, this method keeps track of its progress through each step of computation;

- **Stability**: Once selected as a pivot, elements are always kept sorted above or below their value within the partitioned array. There is no need for further comparisons once you have divided your data into groups based on their order within each group (elements will remain sorted within groups).

Time Complexity of Quicksort

Following along, you should have concluded that quicksort is an O(nlogn) sorting algorithm. This may not seem good since we were hoping for something in O(n), but let's not be too quick to judge. Quicksort has two main advantages over bubble sort and insertion sort.

First, quicksort is an in-place sorting algorithm, meaning that no extra space is required beyond what was used beforehand with the unsorted data set. For example, if you wanted to sort an array with

100 elements using quicksort, you would only need 100 + 1 (the size of your sorted array) bytes of memory. At the same time, if bubble sort or insertion sort were used, then 400 bytes would be needed due to their non-in-place nature (400 being the amount of space needed for one complete pass through a sorted list). Secondly, unlike bubble and insertion sorts which take O(n) time on average, where n represents how long your unsorted list is. On average, Quicksort takes only O(nlogn) time, where logn represents how many swaps or comparisons there are for each pivot value between iterations until no more exchanges occur because all elements are at least as big as their parent!

Advantages of Quicksort

Quicksort is a divide and conquer sorting algorithm, which breaks the input array into two parts, sorts them, and then merges the two sorted arrays. This process is repeated until you end up with one value: the sorted array!

Quicksort has some advantages over other sorting algorithms:

- It's a stable sort; that means if you sort an already-sorted array, it will remain sorted after the quicksort passes through it. This property makes it ideal for situations where you have to sort a lot of data regularly (like in simulations or game AI) because you don't have to worry about your results becoming jumbled when using another sorting method on top of quicksort output.

- Quicksort is also faster than many other sorting algorithms when the input array is already sorted or nearly sorted. This makes it ideal for situations where you have to sort a lot of data regularly (like in simulations or game AI) because you don't have to worry about your results becoming jumbled when using another sorting method on top of quicksort output.

Disadvantages of Quicksort

- Although Quicksort is a fast-sorting algorithm, it also has some disadvantages. The first and foremost disadvantage of Quicksort is that it is not stable. It sorts the elements of an array into non-decreasing order but does not maintain the relative order of two elements with equal values in case they are already sorted. As a result, if you insert an element into an already sorted array, this new element may jump to another position in sorted order compared to where it was before insertion.

- Another disadvantage of Quicksort is that its performance depends on the data distribution and runs slowly on large datasets or those with a high degree of randomness in their elements' values. Because then, there will be many cases where pivot selection doesn't work well and can lead to suboptimal results. One pivot chooses all items greater than itself (left side), while another chooses all items less than itself (right side). This happens when there are not enough items close enough together, so either end must be cut off by a pivot value chosen at random. This reduces effectiveness since only half as much data needs are considered on each side because they don't overlap anymore!

Chapter 6

Heapsort

Heapsort is a sorting algorithm that was developed in 1960. It has been popular because it allows you to sort large lists quickly using little memory. Heapsort works by creating a heap (or pile) out of your list. Then it uses another heap to sort the list.

What Is Heapsort?

Heapsort is a sorting algorithm that uses a heap data structure to sort data. A comparison-based sorting algorithm operates on elements in the array, compares them to each other, and then rearranges them accordingly.

Heapsort works by repeatedly removing the largest element in the array and placing it at the end until the entire array is sorted.

Analysis of Heapsort

Heapsort is a comparison sort, meaning that it compares two numbers at a time and makes decisions based on those comparisons. It's an in-place sort, meaning that it does not require additional memory to do its work; instead, data is rearranged in place within the array being sorted. Heapsort is also a stable sort (unlike

Quicksort), meaning duplicates are kept in the same order before sorting began. Finally, Heapsort runs in linear time (unlike Quick select).

With these characteristics combined with fast swapping times and efficient implementation, Heapsort consistently performs as well as other sorting algorithms when tested against random inputs. Its worst-case performance still beats most other algorithms on average because of its rapid swapping speed and linear-time performance on large inputs.

The algorithm works by repeatedly swapping the smallest element of the subarray with the last element in its parent array. It then compares the new last element with other elements in its parent array (starting at p1) until they are out of order. Once this has occurred, Heapsort moves on to another subarray until all subarrays have been sorted.

Heapsort in Practice

One of the most common applications for Heapsort is sorting data. Heapsort is used to sort data by many applications, including search engines and indexes. A search engine uses an algorithm called 'heapsort' to find out where a user wants to go on the internet based on what they type into the search bar. The index is an internal database that contains all the information about your web pages, like their titles, descriptions, images, etc. It needs to be updated often with new content, so it can be quickly retrieved when someone searches for something related to your website/company name or even just its URL address (e.g., [https://www..com/yourwebsite)

The index is the backbone of your website, so it must always be up-to-date with fresh content.

Heapsort is an algorithm that can be used to sort data. It's similar to quicksort, but instead of sorting the data in place, it uses a 'heap' structure, allowing it to take up less memory space than other sorting algorithms (e.g., quicksort).

Advantages of Heapsort

The following are some of the advantages of Heapsort:

- It's the fastest sorting algorithm for large data sets.

- It's a stable sort, meaning it preserves equal keys' order. A comparison-based sorting algorithm (like Insertion Sort or Bubble Sort) will swap two items with equal keys in its output. If you want only one copy of each key in your output and not just their relative order, use Heapsort instead.

- It's a good choice for sorting large lists on an array because it doesn't move any elements around during its execution, unlike other sorts. For example, Quick Sort and Merge Sort require temporary storage space created by shifting elements into new locations during each iteration.

Disadvantages of Heapsort

The main disadvantage of Heapsort is that it's not a practical sorting algorithm. It takes O(n log n) time, and it's not stable— meaning that if the input contains duplicates, they won't be sorted properly.

When to Use Heapsort

Heapsort is useful when you need to sort a list of elements, but the list length is unknown. This means there is no way of knowing how many elements are in the collection before you start sorting it. In this case, Heapsort will be much faster than other algorithms because it doesn't have to search through all your data simultaneously. Instead, it works on one or two elements simultaneously and builds up its sorted result as it goes along.

Heapsort is a good algorithm when you have a list of elements already in order but need to sort them again for some reason. However, it's not useful if you want the list sorted from start to finish because it takes more steps than other algorithms.

What to Avoid When Using Heapsort

You should never use Heapsort with a list that contains more than one element. As we've discussed, it's not guaranteed that you'll finish sorting the list in order; if it takes too long to compare each element, the algorithm won't be able to finish before the program runs out of memory (or time).

How Does Heapsort Work?

Heapsort is a comparison sort. It uses a heap data structure to store and sort the list in place. This means that the original list is not modified; new nodes are added alongside old ones as they are sorted. This makes Heapsort an in-place O(n log n) algorithm: it takes time proportional to the size of your input (n) and logarithmic time on average (n log n). As with most sorting algorithms, it's important to choose some good data structures so that you don't waste too much memory or processing power during your run through your dataset.

Heapsort Helps Sort Lists Very Fast

Heapsort is a sorting algorithm that works on the principle of placing elements in a list in order of their magnitude. Therefore, the heapsort algorithm is guaranteed to run in O(n log n) time, where n represents the number of elements within the list. This means that as long as your data set is not too big, it will be sorted quickly!

Real-Life Example of Heapsort

Let's take a look at how heapsort works with the help of an analogy.

Suppose you have a list of TV shows you want to watch, sorted in order of popularity (most popular to least popular). The most popular TV show is at the top of the heap, and the least popular TV show is at the bottom.

You would probably want to watch the most popular TV show first, so you would remove it from the heap and put it in your "to watch" list. Then, you would move the next most popular TV show to the top of the heap until there are no more TV shows on the heap.

The result would be a list of TV shows sorted from most popular to least popular. Heapsort is similar to this process, except that instead of TV shows, we sort a list of numbers (or any other type of data).

To understand how heapsort works, we must first understand what a heap is. A heap is a tree-like data structure where each node has two child nodes (left and right). The root node is always at the top, and all other nodes are either greater than or equal to their parent node (if it exists) or less than or equal to their parent node.

Heaps can be either max heaps or min heaps. All nodes are greater than or equal to their child nodes in a max heap. In a min heap, all nodes are less than or equal to their child nodes. For our example above, we want a min heap because we want the smallest element at the top of the heap (in this case, the most popular TV show).

Now that we know what a heap is, let's take a look at how heapsort works step-by-step:

1. We start by building a min heap from our list of numbers (or any other data type). This means we need to rearrange our list to satisfy the conditions for being a min-heap.

2. Once our min heap is built, we can remove the root element (which will always be the smallest element in our list) and put it in its correct position in our sorted list. In our example

above, this would be putting the most popular TV show on our "to watch" list.

3. We then need to reheapify our remaining elements so that they satisfy the conditions for being a min-heap. This means we must rearrange our remaining elements to form a valid min heap.

4. We continue steps 2 and 3 until there are no more elements in our min heap and our list is fully sorted.

  - Note: For step 2 above (removing root element), there are different ways of doing this, depending on whether you're using an array or linked list to store your data.

  - Note: For step 3 above (reheapifying remaining elements), there are different ways of doing this depending on whether you're using an array or linked list to store your data.

When Should You Use Heapsort?

Heapsort might be a good choice if you have enough memory and are not worried about worst-case runtime complexity. However, if you're looking for something with better worst-case runtime complexity, then quicksort might be a better choice since its runtime complexity in the worst-case scenario is $O(\log n)$.

Maintaining the Heap Property

It's easy to struggle to keep your heaps in a logarithmic structure without breaking the heap property. This is especially true if you add elements onto an already-formed heap and must bubble them up through the existing structure. Fortunately, there is an algorithm that helps us do just that.

The heap property is a partial ordering that applies to any binary relation. The heap property is violated if the relation is not a partial ordering.

A heap is a binary tree where each node has at most one parent, except for the root, which has no parent (it's the only node).

The nodes are sorted in ascending order by their keys. The value at each node is less than or equal to the values of its children if any.

Keeping the Heap Property in Check

The heap property is the key to heaps. It's what makes them so useful, and it's a property that all elements in a heap should satisfy: no element can be smaller than any of its children.

The heap property makes it easy to find the minimum element in a heap because you just need to compare each element with its children. For example, suppose an element has children smaller than itself (and therefore not part of the heap). In that case, that element must be larger than those new elements that are now part of the original sorted data set but still smaller than themselves. Since no further comparison levels are needed, there can only be one maximum value per level!

The Simplest Case

Let's say you have a set of heap elements and want to add a new one. In this case, you only need to bubble up the new item until it is in its proper location. This requires comparing the new element with its parent; if they are out of order, swap them and continue doing so until the element is in place.

The same idea can be applied to bubble down. So, for example, if you have a set of heap elements and want to remove the largest one, you need only bubble up until you find it and pop it off the stack.

Keep Heaps in a Logarithmic Structure

We can keep heaps in a logarithmic structure to maintain the heap property.

A heap is a binary tree with the following properties:

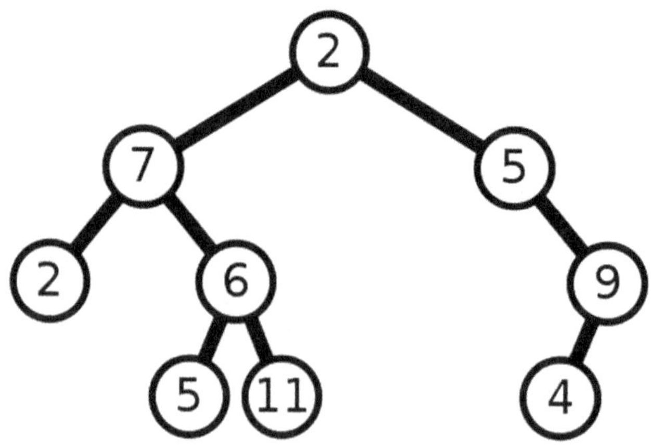

- The number of levels of an n-node binary tree is O(log n).

- For any node x, the value of its children satisfies the key ordering property (i.e., if parent's key < child's key, then parent must be on the right; otherwise, it must be on the left).

The key ordering property assures that all operations preserve the heap property. For example, if we remove a node from a heap, we must replace it with its child whose key is greater than or equal to the parent. This replacement preserves the heap property because it maintains the ordering of nodes in levels, and all nodes of a lower level than x are on the left side of x.

In conclusion, the heap property is useful for understanding dynamic data structures. In addition, it can be used to implement other data structures, like priority queues and heapsort.

Chapter 7

Linear Time Sorting

First, we will go over counting sort. Counting Sort is a sorting algorithm that uses the frequency of each element to determine where it should be placed in the sorted array. It works by counting the number of times each element appears in the unsorted array and then placing it at that location after sorting is complete. This algorithm is also called Radix Sort because it's designed to use certain properties of computers that are limited when compared to our brains (which can do things like add numbers by thinking about them). For example, computers cannot add two numbers together without having them stored somewhere first; this makes counting sort much faster than other algorithms we'll discuss later because there's no need for temporary storage space!

The first step involves taking something called an index variable—a number that denotes which item there are so many copies of—and zeroing out all but one instance each time until all items have been counted only once or twice. Some items may appear more than once, but these can be ignored. Next, break up this list into groups based on how many copies exist within each group (called buckets).

For example: if you wanted your list [4 4 1 6 8 5 2] sorted into ascending order using this method, then your buckets would look like [0 2 4 6 8]. Then simply compare each element in your bucket against its corresponding value from above until you find one with fewer elements than its left neighbor and right neighbor combined; in other words: `x < x + y < x + y + z.` As soon as one such pair has been found, insert these two elements into respective slots before continuing onto another bucket; continue doing so until none remain!

Lower Bounds for Sorting

The worst-case upper bound for sorting is $O(n^2)$, which means that the algorithm will take an exponential amount of time to run on an input array of size n. As a result, this strategy is not very practical in any real-world situation.

The best case (best possible) upper bound is $O(1)$, but achieving this efficiency level is difficult because it requires a lot of work upfront before you can even start sorting. Only two strategies meet this requirement: counting sort and radix sort. They both involve creating and removing subarrays while preserving the order in which items are physically sorted within them—an operation that cannot be performed efficiently in parallel as long as only one computer has access to all information needed at once! So, we need some way around that problem before discussing using either technique effectively within our programs.

Radix Sort

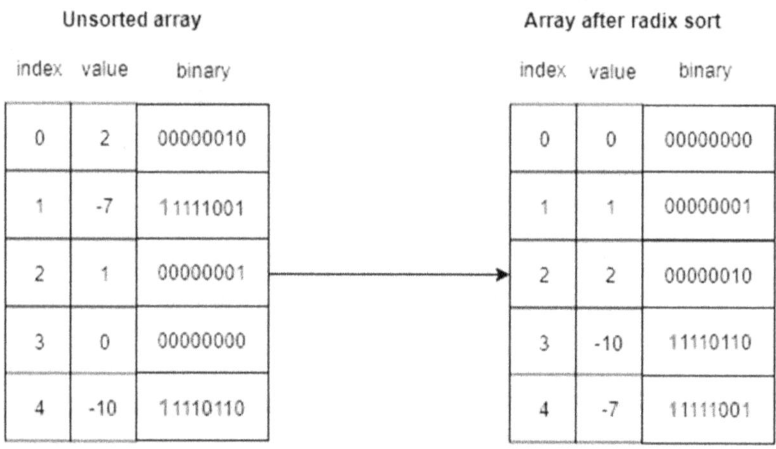

Radix sort is a sorting algorithm that sorts data by their digits in a radix. It can be used to sort numbers, but you can also use it to sort integers, characters, and strings of any length. For example, suppose your data is an array of 10 character/integer strings (each containing at least one digit). In that case, you could use radix sorting to order them alphabetically by their characters. The idea behind this algorithm is that we have a representation for all the values we want to sort. This representation uses each value's position within its own set, its sign (negative or positive), and some base number greater than 0 but less than 1.

Radix Sort Is a Non-Comparative Sorting Algorithm

Radix sort is a non-comparative sorting algorithm. It operates by grouping digits of values and then sorting the groups in ascending order. Radix sort does not require that the strings be sorted before processing; it produces a sorted list directly from the input data.

A Positional Notation Is Required. However, Radix Sort Isn't Limited to Integers, Because We Can Use Integers to Represent Character Strings (Names, Dates, etc.) and Floating-Point Numbers Which Are Specifically Formatted

You will also probably find that the radix sort is useful for all sorts of other things that are not numbers, such as strings and dates. You might wonder what makes Radix sort much better than a simple linear search algorithm.

The answer lies in the use of a positional notation system. A positional notation system allows us to represent numbers by their position in a string of digits. The most commonly used positional notation systems are binary and base 10 (decimal), but there are others, such as octal (base 8) and hexadecimal (base 16).

The Running Time of Radix Depends on the Number of Digits and Equals O(Kn), Where K Is the Length of a Digit

As you might have guessed, Radix Sort is a very efficient sorting algorithm. The running time depends on the number of digits and equals O(kn), where k is the length of a digit. This means that if you compare it to other sorting algorithms, it runs faster than any others. Here's how they stack up:

```
$\mathcal{O}(n)\text{-}$ Insertion Sort
(slowest)

$$\mathcal{O}(\log n)\text{-}$$ Quick Sort
(fastest) $$\mathcal{O}(\frac{\log n}{k})$$
Radix Sort (very fast)
```

Radix Sort Is Fast, But It Is Not Stable

Radix sort is fast, but it is not stable. It sorts data with integer keys by grouping keys by the individual digits which share the same significant position and value. For example, if you have to sort a list of numbers like:

```
1,2,3,4,5
```

The algorithm will group them in a way so that they look like this:

```
1 - 2 - 3 - 4 - 5
```

In conclusion, radix sort is an efficient sorting algorithm that can be used to sort strings and integers. The algorithm is not stable, but its running time is small because no comparisons are required. Radix sort can also be implemented using different representations, such as floating-point numbers or characters.

Bucket Sort

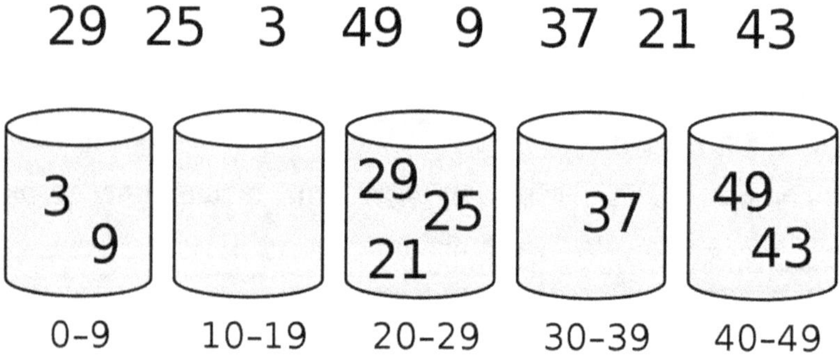

Bucket Sort is a sorting algorithm using divide and conquers to sort items in linear time. It works by dividing the list into smaller lists, sorting each of them, and then combining them back into the original list.

This algorithm can be used to sort an array of numbers (or any other data type that supports comparison) as follows: First, we create a set of buckets equal to the size of our list. Then we take each element and find which bucket it belongs to (comparisons). Finally, after all the elements are assigned their correct bucket index, we can merge all buckets into one (sorted) linked list/array/whatever you want to call it!

Buckets sort is a simple sorting algorithm. It sorts an array by dividing it into buckets and sorting each bucket independently. Buckets are formed by comparing the key of each element to the keys of elements in other buckets. If two keys are equal, they must be swapped before proceeding with further comparisons until no more swapping is necessary or all buckets have been sorted individually.

Pseudocode

- The user will enter a list of numbers.

- The algorithm will create an array of buckets and fill it with the input data (numbers).

- Then, the algorithm will iterate through each element within the array, compare it to one of the available buckets, and then place it into that bucket if they match. Once all elements have been sorted into their respective buckets, we can simply read them out in order using a simple for loop or something similar.

Implementation

The implementation of Bucket Sort is a linked list of lists. Each element in the original array is placed into one of the buckets, and each bucket contains only elements with values less than or equal to that bucket's index. Once all elements are sorted, you can use any sorting algorithm to get them back into their original order.

For example, if you had an array of numbers like [1,2,3] and you wanted to sort it using Bucket Sort such that your result was: [1,[2],3], then your algorithm would look something like this:

1. Create a linked list containing 1 element: mylist = [[]]

2. Add all items from the original array into mylist

3. While there are still items remaining in the original array: If the current item's value < 3, then add the current item at the beginning of mylist; otherwise, add a current item at the end of mylist

4. Return mylist

This algorithm is simple and easy to understand, but it's also rather inefficient. It requires multiple passes over the original array and lots of memory space because we need to store each item twice: once in the linked list and once in its original position within the array.

Performance Analysis

Performance analysis is important in software engineering. It allows you to understand the performance of your program and identify ways to improve it.

Bucket sort is faster than bubble sort but slower than quick sort and merges sort.

Bucket Sort Works Best on Integers, Floating-Point Numbers, and Objects That Can Be Compared Where the Range of Possible Values Is Known

Bucket sort works best on integers, floating-point numbers, and objects that can be compared where the range of possible values is known. For example, you could use bucket sorting to sort a list of student grades from lowest to highest. If your data were floating point numbers and each number was between 0 and 100, you could use bucket sorting to sort them into groups of 100.

Bucket sort works by dividing an array into smaller arrays called "buckets" and then repeatedly moving elements from one bucket to another for as long as elements are in any given bucket. The final step is to merge all the buckets into one large array again in ascending order!

You Can Sort in Linear Time!

But don't let this make you think of sorting as something slow and tedious, like cleaning the kitchen or doing your taxes. Sorting is one of the most fundamental problems in computer science, and many algorithms are built around it. You might have heard about sorting algorithms before; they're used to organize data so that it's easier for programs to understand and work with, especially when a lot of data is involved.

Chapter 8

Order Statistics and Medians

Order Statistics

Order statistics are the first, second, third, and so on. These can be used to find the median. The median is the middle value of a dataset, so it will not be affected by outliers.

- The order statistic corresponding to 50% of your data is the median.

- If there are an even number of values in your dataset, take half of them and add them up, then split them into two groups based on how many values they contain. Call these groups A and B, respectively; calculate their medians separately and find out which one is greater than the other (this will always be true). Finally, add those two medians to get your final result for your mean average!

Min and Max

The min and max functions return the smallest and largest values in a dataset, respectively. Using these functions, you can find the range of your dataset.

For example, if we wanted to find the minimum value in [1,2,3], we could use min (1,2,3), which would return 1.

Similarly, if you wanted to find the maximum value in [1,2], you would use max (1).

When N Is Odd

When n is odd, the median is the middle value of the data set. This can be calculated by dividing the total number of values in a set into two halves and taking their average.

The formula for finding the median is as follows: (n+1)/2, the element of the data set when it is placed into order. In other words, the median is the value exactly in the middle of a data set when sorted from lowest to highest.

When N Is Even

When a data set has an even number of elements, the median equals the average of the two middle elements. For example, if you want to find out what the median of {1,2,3,4} is, then you would calculate

```
median = (2+3)/2 = 2.5
```

The median can be considered a value that divides your data into two equal parts. So, if your dataset had only one element, it wouldn't have been able to divide itself into two equal parts, so there would be no median value for this case. The same goes for any set with three or more elements under consideration where all members in each half can't be at an equal distance from each other (like in our example above).

There are ways around these limitations by using percentiles instead, but we'll leave those aside here because they're unnecessary when discussing medians!

Median of Medians Algorithm

So, what is the median of the median algorithm?

It's a way to find the median value of an array or set of numbers. The key idea is that if you have an array, you can compute its middle item based on two other arrays: one containing all but one and all but two values. If your array has an even number of items (for example, 2 or 4), both these subarrays are equal to half their length. Thus, they contain exactly half as many elements as your original array. Each element in each subarray thus also represents 1/2nth place in the sorted order of all elements in that subarray, which means we can find their median by just averaging them together!

Order Statistics Form the Foundation for Building a Good Algorithm for Finding the Median, Which Can Be Used for Other Purposes

Order Statistics form the foundation for building a good algorithm for finding the median, which can be used for other purposes. The order statistics are simply the data that is sorted and is present at both ends of an array (or set). For example, suppose we have a list of 10 numbers as 1, 2, 3, 4, 5, 6, 7, 8, and 9. If we sort this list from lowest to highest, our order statistics would be 1 and 10. However, if we sort them from highest to lowest, our order statistics would be 10 and 1.

Selection in Expected Linear Time

The algorithm requires O (1) space, meaning that you can use it in any situation where the size of your data structure is fixed. This is usually a good thing since it means you won't have to worry about reallocating memory every time you run your program. It also means that if a machine has 1 GB of RAM and wants to run this algorithm on 2 MB worth of data, it will still be able to do so without worrying about running out of memory!

The algorithm runs in O (1) time complexity: literally, zero seconds, no matter how big or small your input set is! This makes sense given that only two steps are involved: pick one element from each subset at random; then return all elements whose indices were picked (namely those belonging to subsets containing those ids). If these two steps take less than 1 second each, then we know their combined complexity must also be less than 1 second (since adding two numbers together takes less than one second). Since picking an element at random takes no time, and neither does returning it, this gives us our final result, which says, "The algorithm executes in 0 seconds."

Selection in Worst-Case Linear Time

In the worst-case scenario, selection may take linear time. This can be accomplished using random pivot points to select elements from an array. In the average case scenario, this implementation performs better than one based on sorting because it preserves the locality of reference on each iteration through the data set.

Unordered Array Implementation of Selection

Here's how to find the median of an unordered array:

- Assign an index to each item in the array, starting at 0 and ending with n-1.

- Find the pivot element, which is any value that doesn't equal any other value and has a lower index than all elements with higher indices. It's usually easiest to look at all possible values, then go through them again, looking for one that doesn't match anything else and isn't higher than any other value. If you've found a unique value that matches this description, mark it as your pivot element; otherwise, keep going until you find one or run out of items in your list (or both).

- Swap the pivot element with its right neighbor (or left if you're working with zero-based arrays). This will move two or three elements depending on whether two or three objects are larger than your pivot point. If there are only two larger items (as was true in our example), then you don't need to do any additional swapping because these two elements will now be next to each other without anyone else between them. If there were three larger items before swapping occurs—assuming none of those items were swapped—then after exchanging places between #3 & #4 (or #4 & #5), we'll have four distinct groups consisting of exactly one item each!

- We can repeat this process as often as necessary until no more swaps occur. Each time we do so, we'll cut down on our search space exponentially while increasing efficiency by reducing the time spent searching every permutation individually through brute force methods like comparing every pair against every other pair."

Ordered Array Implementation of Selection

The ordered array implementation of selection is similar to the randomized one, with two crucial differences:

- The first element in the array is selected as the pivot point. This makes sense if you consider that all elements in a worst-case linear time algorithm can be already sorted.

- The index of the pivot point is found by calculating its median value (if there are an odd number of elements in your array).

Selection Can Be Made in Linear Time By Using Random Pivot Points, Which Allows for a Faster Average Case Scenario

The worst-case scenario for selection is still an O(n) operation, but the average case is much faster. This is because the average case becomes O (1), which means that after 1 iteration of this algorithm, you've already done as much work as you will on any given input size.

For Example:

Let's say our list has 10 items (x1 through x10). If we select a random pivot point of 0 and then insert all the items into sorted order after that pivot point, then 9 times out of 10, we'll have a sorted list with 2 or 3 comparisons per item. The other tenth of the time, we'll end up with an unsorted list since sometimes our first insertion will fail due to duplicate values or whatnot--but again, this only happens about 1/10th of the time.

As we saw above, the average case is always equal to or smaller than the worst-case scenario. In this case, we can see that if an array of integers were sorted in ascending order, random pivot points would allow us to select any given integer in linear time and with no more than two comparisons. This means that even though the worst-case scenario requires at least $O(n)$ operations and comparisons before finding a given element (if it exists), we only need $O(1)$ operations and comparisons on average.

Chapter 9

Hash Tables

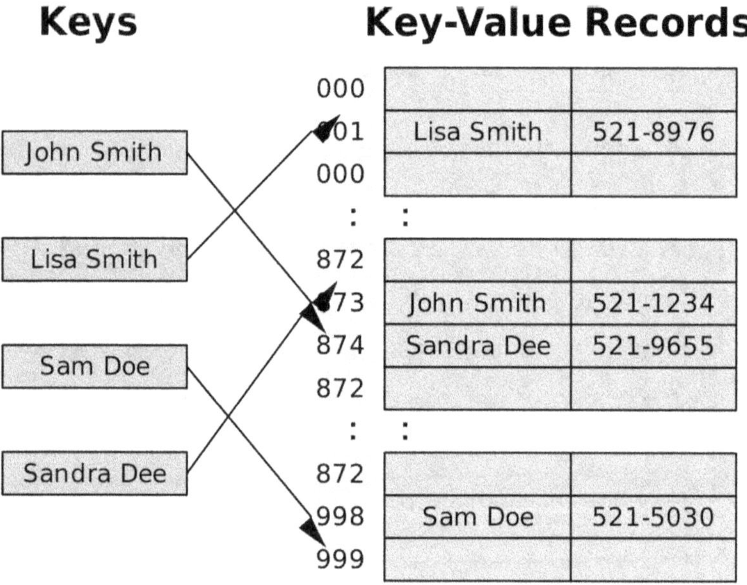

Have you ever had to store key-value pairs in your program? If so, chances are you used a hash table. Hash tables are data structures that can be used to quickly search for and retrieve values based on the keys they are associated with. They're particularly useful when you have large amounts of data that require quick access, such as in games or simulations where you need to find certain items quickly or in databases where you want to look up specific records based on criteria.

Hashing Collisions

Hash tables use the hash function to convert the key into an integer value. Since there are no guarantees that every key will have a unique hash, two different keys can produce the same value. Your program must handle these collisions, and they can occur in several ways:

- There might be two different keys with identical hashes, both of which map to the same bucket in the table.

- There might be two different keys with identical hashes where only one maps to a bucket in the table; this would cause an unnecessary collision if you had used a less efficient hashing technique like linear probing (instead of quadratic probing). This collision would happen much more often than here because each value would only have one opportunity to match any given key's hash value instead of four such opportunities.

Storing Key-Value Pairs

When you store key-value pairs in a hash table, each key-value pair is called a "bucket." The buckets are linked together in a chain. When you add a new key-value pair, it is also added to the chain.

If you have an existing hash table with 100 keys and values and add another value, there will be 101 entries! This may sound inefficient, but remember that we're working with an array of linked lists here—and it turns out that these arrays can grow very large without taking up too much memory space.

The hash table is useful because it allows us to store and retrieve items quickly. For example, let's say we want to find the value associated with a particular key—we simply use an algorithm called "linear probing" (or some other technique) that allows us to search through the chain of linked lists until we find it.

When we add a new value to the hash table, we must ensure that it fits in with the existing keys and values. The most common way of doing this is called "linear probing." Linear probing works by starting at one end of the array of linked lists and searching through them one by one until we find an empty spot where our new key-value pair can fit in.

If we can't find an empty spot, we simply split one of the linked lists in two by inserting our new key-value pair. If the array has been properly balanced (which is why we need those extra pointers), then this will cause all the other linked lists to get smaller by one entry each—making room for our new entry.

Let's take a look at how this works. Suppose we want to add the key-value pair (1, 2) into our hash table. We start by searching through each linked list until we find an empty spot where our new key-value pair can fit in.

If we find an empty spot, we insert our new key-value pair into it. If not, we split one of the linked lists in two by inserting our new key-value pair.

This will cause all the other linked lists smaller by one entry each—making room for our new entry.

Hash Tables in Clojure, Python, C++, And Java

Hash tables are a very common data structure that can store key-value pairs. They are used in many languages, such as Python and C++. One of the reasons hash tables are so commonly used is because they have an efficient lookup time.

For example, if you wanted to store the names and ages of your friends, you could use a Java HashSet class which stores keys and values together in one collection. Every time you want to find someone's age, you must pass their name into the set as a key and get their age as a value!

Hash Tables Store Key-Value Pair Data and Can Be Found in Many Languages

Hash tables operate on a set of keys, each key being an integer that is mapped to an associated value. Hash tables are often used in place of arrays and linked lists because they can more efficiently store the same data. Of course, the exact algorithm for choosing the location where any given item is stored depends on the programming language used. Still, it's usually based on a hash function that produces an integer output.

The hash table stores key-value pairs in locations called buckets, which are typically fixed size (though this can vary). Each bucket contains several items from any given "set" of values. The process of determining whether a certain value exists in a hash table begins by generating an index based on its key using the appropriate hash function. If this index falls within a valid range for your bucket sizes (e.g., [0..1000] or [0..100]), then you know that your item does not exist; otherwise, you can proceed with looking up its location using just its index!

Hash tables are useful because they allow you to store data without worrying about where it will be stored. This means that you can add new items at any time, and it doesn't matter if the number of items already in the hash table changes over time.

As an example, consider a hash table that stores key-value pairs for words in the English language. It would be pretty easy to add new words as long as they were valid English words; you wouldn't have to worry about where they should go or how many other keys were already there!

Direct-Address Tables

Direct-address tables are a fast way to look up data, but they can be wasteful of space and don't work well for all types of keys.

Searching in a Direct-Address Table Is Fast, But the Table Itself Can Be Wasteful of Memory

A direct-address table is an array of data where each element has a unique key value. The keys are used to look up the value in the array. A direct-address table can be searched with an efficient binary search algorithm. Still, because it uses a single large array as its index (the key), it consumes as much memory as the total number of items stored in the table.

To add new items to a direct-address table:

- Find an unused slot for your new entry by searching for its key value.

- Insert your entry into this slot and update pointers if necessary (for example, if you used sequential access).

To access an item in a direct-address table: Look up its key value by running a binary search algorithm. Then, retrieve the associated data from memory and return it to the caller.

Inserting into a Direct-Address Table Is Fast, But It May Cause the Table to Fill Up Quickly, Causing High Memory Usage

Inserting values into a direct-address table is fast, but it can cause the table to fill up quickly.

Memory usage will be proportional to the number of entries in the table and the number of bits used to represent each entry (which could be different for each key). If any of your keys are similar, they may share a common prefix. In this case, you can use an array instead because arrays allow you to specify different lengths for different keys while still using just one array.

The Free Direct-Addressing Scheme Will Not Work for Keys in a Range of Numbers Rather Than a Set of Numbers Like the Example Above

The free direct-addressing scheme will not work for keys in a range of numbers rather than a set of numbers like the example above. This is because the table can only hold one entry per key, and if the number range is large enough, you would need more entries than possible keys. For instance, if you had 250 billion possible keys (and we'll assume they're all equally likely), your table would need to be 250 billion entries long! Because this is impossible, we must resort to other methods of storing information about our keys. These include hash functions and b-trees. Both these methods offer excellent storage utilization while still being fast enough for most applications (hash functions are slower than b-trees).

A Direct-Address Table Can Be Wasteful of Space and Not Work Well for All Types of Keys

For example, suppose you have a direct-address table that allows you to look up customers by their social security number. If the customers' social security numbers are all in the same range, from 1001 through 9999, this table would be fast for searching but not so good for inserting new customer records.

If each customer has a unique social security number and you want to allow the user to search by any portion of the social security number (for example, someone might only know part of their SSN). Then this kind of direct-address table would be fine. But if each customer's SSN is unique and has no relationship with other SSNs, then it would waste space having all those individual entries under one key (in this case, "1001"). Furthermore, this wasted space could cause problems if there were more records than expected (due to errors in entering data).

Direct-address tables are a good solution if you know in advance that your key values will be of a fixed size and if you also need to search for them quickly. However, they don't work so well when the number range is too large or if there are many different keys with differing amounts of memory usage needed.

Perfect Hashing

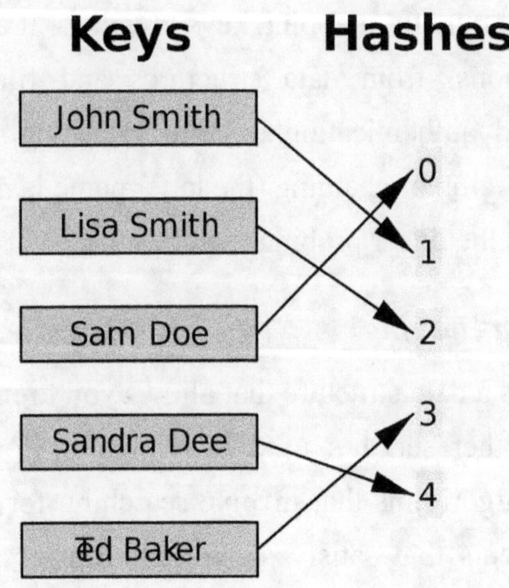

Hash functions are an important part of any programming language and have various uses.

Perfect hashing is a clever technique for implementing a hash table where the number of elements in the table and the size of each element are limited. It works by using an auxiliary array to store additional information about each key, but only if it's needed.

This approach is called perfect hashing because it turns an arbitrarily large set of keys into an unlimited number of hash tables that can be created based on their contents. Perfect hashing also allows you to use any type of key as long as there is some way to compare elements without knowing what they are (e.g., strings or integers).

Introduction and Definition

Hashing is a technique for mapping keys to values. It can be used in various applications, from data structures and file systems to cryptography and authentication systems. Hashing is sometimes referred to as indexing or chaining (the latter name is more common when referring to the linear probing method).

History of Perfect Hashing

Perfect hashing is a data structure that allows you to map keys from one set into another set. It's used in computers to improve the performance of algorithms that involve searching for data, such as finding all elements that satisfy some condition or sorting items based on specific criteria.

Robert Tarjan invented perfect hashing in 1979 while working at Bell Labs.

Let's say you have a set of keys (elements) and want to store them in an ordered list:

```
[1, 2, 3]
```

The obvious solution would be to create an array with three positions:

```
[1][2].[3]
```

If you wanted to add another element—say 4—you could simply add a fourth position:

```
[1][2].[3][4]
```

However, if your list had hundreds or thousands of elements and needed frequently updating because they frequently change as well., this would become impractical very quickly!

Types of Hash Functions and Use-Cases

A hash function is a procedure that maps data of arbitrary size to fixed-size data. Hash functions are used in many applications, including databases and computer security. This article introduces the theory behind hashing and its use in programming.

Hashing is one of the most commonly used cryptographic primitives, so much so that we take it for granted in everyday life; consider your credit card number as an example: when you swipe your card at a store or restaurant, what happens behind the scenes?

Your credit card company has stored all its customers' data (including their names) and a unique ID associated with each customer. Whenever someone swipes their card through payment processing equipment, they receive back only their unique ID. this is known as de-duplication or deduplication. Here identical pieces of information are matched against each other to identify which one came first based on some piece of distinguishing property. We can do this because all our credit cards have been given numbers generated by applying a hash function called SHA1 (Secure Hash Algorithm 1) to the customer's name. This means that even though two people may have similar names, like David Smith or David Jones, even if we know exactly who these two people are, there would still be no way for us to know if someone else had already purchased something from us. SHA1 will always produce different hashes for each person's name.

How to Find a Perfect Hash Function for a Given Set?

There are three basic strategies for finding a perfect hash function:

- **Use a known perfect hash function**. There are only a few of these, but they're useful in their own right. They all have the property that if you put any two inputs into them, one of two things happens: either they produce the same output or different outputs. If you want to know more about these functions, google "picklehash" (seriously) and read up on it!

- **Use an almost-perfect hash function**. Most people do this when looking for a perfect hash function; many of these are available online and in books like "The Algorithm Design

Manual." The key thing about using an almost-perfect hash function is that while it may not be random on average, its outputs should still be pretty good across the board. Meaning that any two inputs should produce similar outputs with high probability (which means that if one input produces an output with value X and another produces Y with probability $p > 1/2$). A quick Google search will help here too!

- **Use a near-perfect hashing scheme such as [NuPRL].** These will guarantee even distribution across all possible values (or within order(p). which means that no matter what operation you might perform on your data set before hashing, it should not cause significant change to its overall distribution once hashed by this method. This makes sense since if there were significant changes, we would expect our results to diverge significantly from those obtained using standard statistical tests like chi-square tests (which we do not intend to apply here!).

What Is a Universal Hash Function?

Universal Hashing functions are used to hash every possible input into a fixed-size array. This is done by using a family of hash functions instead of just one single function.

Universal Hash functions are used to store large data in limited memory space.

Ideal Universal Hash Function

A hash function is a function that maps some set of inputs to a fixed-size output. The ideal universal hash function has the following properties:

- It is "universal" because it can be used for any input data set.

- The mapping between inputs and outputs should be one-to-one or singleton. Only one input is mapped to each possible output value and vice versa.

- The mapping should be "distinct," meaning that each input produces a unique output (no two inputs are mapped to the same output).

Hash Functions Are an Important Part of Any Programming Language and Are Extensively Used

Hash functions are an important part of any programming language and are extensively used. For example, they are used to create an index for a data structure, generate checksums, create fingerprints, and generate random numbers.

The basic idea behind hash functions is simple: take the input (a string or number) and return a single value representing it. This value should be unique (or at least very close to unique) across all inputs so we can quickly find them using this value as an index.

Chapter 10

Elementary Data Structures

Data structures are the backbone of any programming language. They provide structure for the data being stored and manipulated, making it easier for you to write code.

Stacks and Queues

Stacks and queues are two of computer science's most fundamental data structures. They're useful for managing a list of items that need to be processed or organized, but for different reasons.

What Is a Stack?

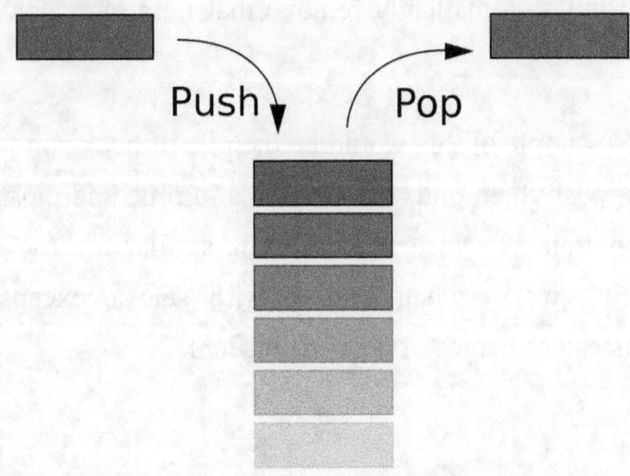

A stack is a data structure that keeps things in order. It's a collection of items, and they're added to the top and removed from the top in reverse order. Put another way: The first item you put on a stack will be the last one you get off; each item has its place in a stack so that you know where it is and where it was when you put it there.

Examples of stacks include dinner plates at a buffet or tools on your workbench - dishes are added to the bottom of the pile while people take them off in order (first comes out, first served). When an object is taken out of its place, it doesn't just fly off into space; instead, someone puts it back where it belongs when they're done using it - like when dinner guests use their forks as skewers for meatballs before handing them over to be washed by waitstaff at some point during dessert service!

How Are Stacks Useful?

A stack is a data structure organizes data in a last-in-first-out (LIFO) manner. A stack will only allow you to access the last item added and will automatically remove that item after you are done using it.

A real-life example of this would be the pile of books on your desk, where you push them onto the top one at a time and pick them off from the bottom one at a time. This is similar to how computer programming works when dealing with stacks, except we use indexes instead of names or other identifiers.

In computer science and C++ programming, there are multiple ways we can implement stacks to store information:

- Using arrays (or any type of container) as our model for storing items;

- Using pointers as our model for storing items;

- Using linked lists as our model for storing items

What Is a Queue?

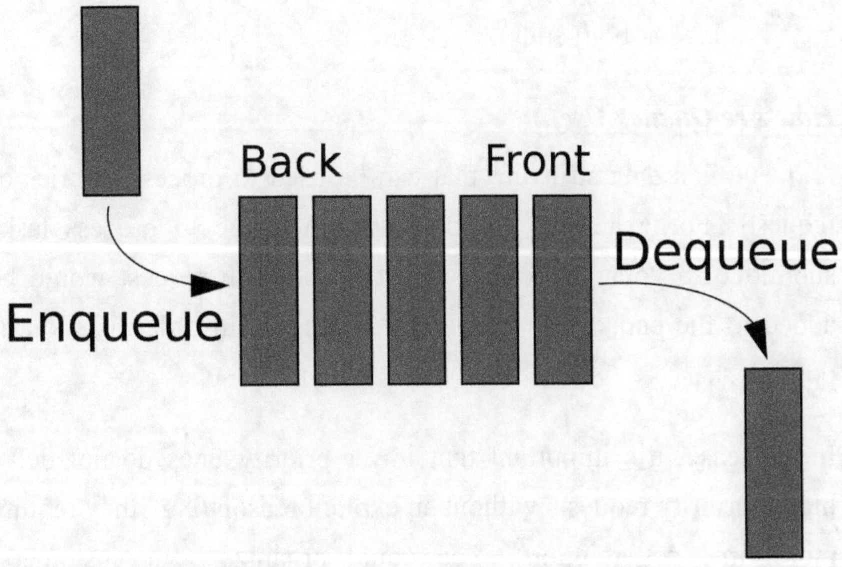

A queue is a data structure that stores elements in the order they are inserted. Elements can be added to the back of the queue, but they are removed from the front.

- In other words, a queue maintains two ends: one for adding new items and one for removing them when needed. Adding items to an empty queue inserts them at the back, and removing items from an empty queue removes them from the front.

- Another way to imagine you have a line at an amusement park, and there's only one open roller coaster car (not enough cars). As people get on, someone has to move their seat forward so another person can sit down because there aren't any available seats in front of them yet (the end where nobody sits). Once everyone has been seated, then those people standing around waiting can get on as well (elements added at both ends).

How Are Queues Useful?

A queue is a data structure that can be used to process a series of requests. For example, you could use a queue to process tasks submitted to your customer support team. Each request would be added to the end of the queue and processed in order as soon as possible.

In this case, it's important that lower priority ones do not delay higher priority requests without an explicit reason (e.g., they require more time or attention). You could organize your customers' requests by assigning them different weights—the heavier the weight, the earlier they should be processed—and use a priority queue with weighted insertions to implement this feature.

A Python implementation of this type of priority queue would look something like this:

```
from collections import OrderedDict def
insert_weighted_item(queue): """Add an item
into `queue` according to its weight""" curr
= OrderedDict () try: curr[queue] += 1
except KeyError: curr[queue] = 1 return
dict(items=curr)
```

Stacks and Queues Are Simple But Powerful Data Structures

Stacks and queues are two of the most commonly used data structures in computer science, and they're very simple to understand. You can use them to manage all kinds of things in your programs, from a list of tasks to a series of events or messages between two people (like text messages!).

They're also easy to implement in different programming languages. This makes stacks and queues useful for many different applications—and since they're so simple, it's easy to learn how they work!

For example, here's how we could implement stacks and queues using Python:

```Python

def get(stack): #
```

Get an element out at the top of the stack. If there aren't any elements left on the stack, raise an error telling us this happened.

```
    return stack[0]
```

In summary, a stack is like a pile of plates: when you add a plate to the top, it pushes the other plates down. Likewise, a queue is like waiting in line at an airport: when someone gets on the plane, everyone else moves up one spot until they're next in line for their board turn. Both data structures are useful because they help us model real-world problems; their simplicity makes them easy to implement!

Representing Rooted Trees

Trees are a very important data structure and have many applications in computer science. They can be represented as rooted trees, which use a single node called the root to point to any other node in a tree. The other nodes are then considered successors of the root, with all unreachable nodes forming a subtree that we call the nullary forest.

A Rooted Tree Is a Directed Edge-Labeled Graph G = (V, E) Where Each Node Has Exactly One Outgoing Edge to a Successor Node, and the Edge Labels Partially Order Nodes

A rooted tree is a directed edge-labeled graph G = (V, E) where each node has exactly one outgoing edge to a successor node, and the edge labels partially order nodes. The root node is the first node in this ordering, and all other nodes have successors.

The Set of All Nodes Reachable from the Root Is Called the Tree

While the set of all nodes reachable from the root is called the tree itself, this set can be empty. In that case, we say it's a nullary or nullary forest.

If you like, you can think of a tree as having two kinds: rooted and unrooted (and their respective subclasses). The roots of rooted trees are their parents, also called nodes or vertices in graph theory.

The Remaining G Nodes Are Unreachable, Forming a Subtree That We Call the Nullary Forest

A nullary forest is the set of all nodes reachable from the root but not from each other. The nullary forest is, therefore, the disjoint union of trees:

- G1 = [(0)]

- G2 = [(1)]

Trees Can Also Be Represented in an Array-Based Fashion

If a tree is represented as an array, then you can use the index of that array to represent nodes in your tree. The value at that index will be used to store edges. For example, here's how you might represent a rooted binary search tree using this technique:

- `TREE = [2 3 5 7 11 13 17 19 23 29 31 37 41 43];`

- `TREE[1] = 2;`

- `TREE[2] = 3;`

- `TREE[3] = 5;`

- `TREE[4] = 7;`

This lets us easily run our algorithms on arrays rather than doing extra work converting between different representations!

Implementing Pointers and Objects

In programming, there are a few fundamental concepts that you need to learn to make sense of the world. These concepts include variables, loops, and conditionals. However, one important concept that is often overlooked is pointers and objects.

What Is a Pointer?

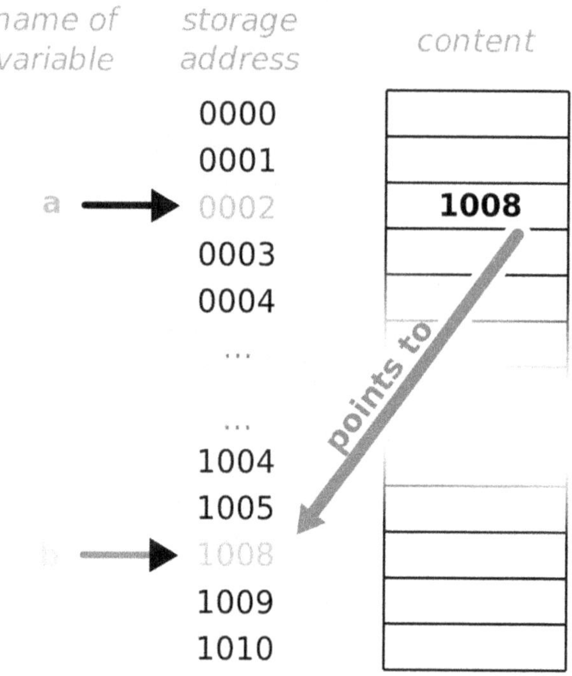

A pointer is a variable that stores the memory address of another variable. It's useful to think of pointers as an array of values, except instead of storing numbers or text, it stores addresses. You can think of this like an address book; if you have a friend named "John Smith," you could store his phone number in your address book by writing down his name and then the digits at which he lives (his phone number). Once you've written this information down, you could use it whenever needed: when someone calls asking for John Smith's number, you would look up their name on your list and give them his digits without getting out any paper. Similarly, when programs want to access data stored in memory (such as all the words inside "my computer"), they use pointers as their way into that data—they just need some way to refer back again later!

Pointers and Objects

Pointers and Objects are two types of variables that store data. Pointers are used to store the memory address of a variable, while Objects are used to store the data of a variable.

How to Implement?

To implement pointers, you must first ensure that the compiler supports them. If they do, then you can declare a pointer variable using the following syntax:

```
int *myPointer;
```

The * means that it is a pointer. The type of data stored in myPointer is an integer denoted by int.

To access the data stored in myPointer, you can use the syntax:

```
myPointer = &myInteger;
```

The & means that it is an address. By assigning it to myPointer, you are telling the compiler to store the address of myInteger into myPointer.

What Are the Advantages of Using Pointers and Objects?

Pointers and objects have many advantages. These include:

- Write more efficient code. Pointers and objects can help you to write more efficient code by reducing the number of instructions required to perform a task or by making it easier to avoid unnecessary copies of data. e.g., avoid using one if you don't need a copy of an array in your program.

- Manage memory effectively. Pointers allow you to hold on to references that point at where actual data is stored in memory, rather than holding on to copies (which may take up space) or references themselves (which might not be as fast). Objects are similar but also allow you accessors faster than traditional variables because they don't require constant dereferencing when accessing data inside them. They use pointers instead — while still allowing the same flexibility as regular instance variables that could otherwise be accessed through object methods instead.

- Make it easier for others' code to re-use yours seamlessly by providing functions for common tasks such as searching arrays for particular elements and generating random numbers. These functions will often return their results via pointers so other programs can use them correctly without knowing how they work internally.

- Allow greater modularization between parts of your program: instead of having a large file with everything in it, use separate files for each module containing functions or classes that perform particular tasks. If someone wants to use one of these functions in another program, they just have to include the file.

Coding becomes much more manageable and less intimidating when you get familiar with pointers and objects. This is partly because pointers and objects can be used for many applications.

For example, you can use them to store information about a person in a database or build an app that mimics Snapchat.

Linked Lists

Linked lists are one of the most fundamental data structures in computer science. They're like a row of storage units with an index number, and you can access them by referencing their index number. Each storage section has a pointer that points to the next section in the list, thus forming a chain. You can add or take out sections without affecting any other part of the chain as long as you don't break any pointers along the way!

Singly-Linked Lists

Singly-linked lists are the most basic linked lists because each element has to store only one pointer to its next element. In a singly linked list, you need to allocate the same amount of space for every node in the list (this is not true for doubly or circularly linked lists). However, if you want to add an element at the end of a directly linked list and you don't have enough space left in your data structure (such as if it were full), then you would need to create another new data structure that holds all of these pointers.

Doubly Linked Lists

The second kind of linked list is a doubly linked list. Each node has two references in a doubly linked list: one to the next node in the list and one to the previous node. This makes it easy to traverse forward and backward through a sequence of nodes.

This kind of data structure is used when you want to keep track of several different things at once. For example, if you're writing an inventory system that records not only what items are in stock but also where they're stored on your warehouse floor (something like "item X is located at spot Y").

Linked Lists Are Useful Data Structures with Different Variations

Linked Lists are one of the most useful data structures in computer science. With their ability to store data that has an order, they are used to create and store many different types of data.

These can be simple things like a list of names or more complicated things like a list of grades on a test. They can also be used for storing lists themselves (linked lists are recursive).

Linked lists are primarily used when you need to store something like a series of numbers or letters in order, with each element following directly after the previous element.

Linked Lists are useful data structures with different variations. Many programming languages use them, and they have many uses. For example, you can use them to store information or even traverse it.

Chapter 11

Binary Search Trees

A binary search tree is a data structure that can store elements, with the property that each element is stored at some node of the tree. This means that each node in a binary search tree may have up to two children (left or right), and no node has more than two children.

All leaves are at the same level, which means there are no other nodes between them and their parents. The root of the tree is always present in every binary search tree. The nodes on any path from this root to an arbitrary node will always be balanced: they form an alternating sequence of left and right branches (each branch also known as a subtree). For example, consider this implementation of a Binary Search Tree:

- Root - {1} / \ {2} - {3} / \ \ \{4} - {5} / \

- In this example, note how each branch has exactly one left branch (or subtree) followed by one right branch (or subtree). This makes our search algorithm efficient because it allows us to determine whether we should go down one side or another quickly once we've found our insertion point within the current branch.

The main advantage of using a binary search tree is that searching for an item within the tree is extremely efficient. This efficiency comes from the fact that each node in a binary search tree has two children, and therefore there are only two possible paths to reach any particular node: left or right (and then up).

Computational Complexity

Now let's look at some common ways this data structure can be implemented and their computational complexity.

- **Linear Search**: This is the simplest way to implement a binary search tree, and it has linear time complexity (meaning that its running time is proportional to the number of elements in the BST). In other words, if you want to find an element within a BST that has n elements total, then it will take n steps (assuming all operations are performed on average).

- **Logarithmic Search**: This method uses more memory than linear search but runs much faster because each operation takes logarithmic time instead of linear time, like linear search. In other words, if you want to find an element within a BST that has n elements total, then it will take $O(\log(n))$ steps (assuming all operations are performed on average).

- **Binary Search**: This method uses less space than its predecessors while having comparable performance characteristics -- meaning that it runs just as fast as either one but takes up less space overall. This makes this algorithm ideal for situations where memory usage needs to decrease without sacrificing speed too much!

It's a little more complicated than the previous two, but it's still a simple algorithm. The first step is to find the middle element in your BST; this will be your pivot point. Then, you can compare each element to this pivot point and its neighbors (the elements above and below it). If an element is greater than or equal to the pivot, it cannot possibly be part of the solution set and must be discarded.

Height

If a binary search tree has n nodes, then the tree's height is defined as the length of its longest path from the root to the leaf. The height of a binary search tree with n nodes will be log2(n).

The time complexity of a binary search tree is O(log n). This is because the average number of comparisons to find an element in a binary search tree is log2(n), so the total number of comparisons done has to be less than or equal to log2(n) times the number of nodes in the tree.

Inserting

Insertion is the act of adding a new node to an existing binary search tree. This is done by comparing the key of the new node to that of its parent and then making the appropriate choice based on whether or not it's less than, equal to, or greater than the parent's key. If this sounds confusing, then don't worry! The leaf nodes of a BST have no other children, so we can insert them easily:

- If `key < x,` we take `x` as our new root node and make `key` be its left child (the first child).

- If `key <= x,` we take `x` as our new root node and make `key` be its right child (the last child).

As you can see from these examples, this algorithm runs in O(log n) time—which means it takes logarithmic steps before returning a result!

Deleting

First, find the node's parent to delete a node from a binary search tree. Then, remove the node and its children.

If the node is not in the tree, return null.

Binary Search Trees Are Data Structures That Are Good for When the Order of the Data Does Not Matter

Binary Search Trees are data structures that are good for when the order of the data does not matter.

Consider a BST of integers:

- The root node stores a value (e.g., 5)

- Every other node in its subtree stores either a smaller or larger value than its parent (e.g., 3, 7)

The values stored in these nodes can be considered pages on an encyclopedia or dictionary: they're ordered by name and alphabetically sorted within each letter group. You probably already know that if you want to find the entry for "cat," you should look under "C" rather than "K."

Binary Search Trees are a data structure that is good for when the order of the data does not matter. They can be used as primary indices in memory and have many applications. Binary Search Trees are also very efficient at searching through data since they only need to look at each item once before they find what they're looking for!

Querying a Binary Search Tree

Binary search trees (BSTs) are data structures that are useful for storing non-sorted data. You can think of them as an ordered list where every node has up to two children. The nodes themselves contain a value and pointers to their children. Searching through a BST is done by comparing each node and the value you are searching for until an exact match is found or there are no more nodes left to compare to your value.

The first thing we need to do when querying our BST is to make sure it's initialized properly:

Initial Conditions

Given the definition of a binary tree and the operations for manipulating it, this is not too hard to do.

First, you must initialize your tree, then add some data.

To initialize an empty binary search tree, you simply create a root node with no children (or null). This will be denoted as T:=T(null), where T is a pointer to any tree node (except the root).

Once you have initialized an empty tree initializing a non-empty one is easy: just choose some key k such that k<x[0]. Then make x[1] equal to either x[0] or x[0]'s right child (it doesn't matter which), depending on whether k<x[1]'s left child or not, respectively; and repeat for each subsequent level until all levels have been filled up completely. Once that's done, every node except for T has two children who are less than them (in terms of their keys) and greater than them, respectively; hence they are correctly placed within the BST structure!

Querying a Binary Search Tree

A query function is a function that takes in a value and returns either true or false. In the context of binary search trees, we'll be using it to check if a node contains the searched-for value.

For example, suppose you have a BST with values {5, 4, 2}. You can use your query function to find out if 3 is present in this structure by calling it on each node (and its children) until you hit one that doesn't return true for your test value:

If 3 isn't present in this tree, q(3) will always return false. And if it does exist somewhere, then it has to be reached via some path from e because e was its parent; therefore, q(4) will also eventually return true for some i such that i > 4 and i < 5

Check If the BST Is Empty

- We can use the [isEmpty](#) method to check if a BST is empty. This method returns true if the BST is empty and false otherwise.

- The [isEmpty()](#) method checks the root node of the BST.

Check If the Value Exists in the Tree

- **Check if the value exists in the left sub-tree**: If the current node has a left child, you will need to recursively check if that node also contains your value. If it does, return true and terminate your recursion. Otherwise, move on to check whether there is another node in this subtree that could contain your value.

- **Check if the value exists in the right sub-tree**: Similar to checking for left children, you will need to recursively check whether any of these nodes contain your value or not. If so, return true and terminate your recursion. Otherwise, push any results up until now onto a new stack data structure. So that you can compare them later on) and continue looking through this new branch of nodes all over again until no more branches exist or one of them contains what we're looking for!

- **Find out if our root node contains our target item**: This step may seem familiar because it's similar to what happens when searching through a list! We simply go through each branch from our root node one by one until we either find something matching our criteria or run out of options completely - but we don't have enough information about binary trees yet to determine which case applies here, so let's keep reading about how they work instead :)

Find the Lowest Value in the Tree

You'll need to write a recursive function to find the lowest value in a binary search tree. The recursive function should take three arguments:

- A node in the binary search tree

- An integer that represents the current depth of recursion (i.e., how many times it has been called)

- A variable to hold the value returned by this recursive call (i.e., what you want your function to return)

The body of this recursive function should do exactly what it says on the tin: We're going to call ourselves with an argument corresponding to each node we encounter as we traverse our way from the root down through all nodes until we reach one that's empty. At that point, we'll return whatever value was stored inside it! If any other type of node is encountered—like one containing some data—then instead, we'll just add its contents onto our result variable and then call ourselves again with another iteration number from here on out. No more empty nodes will be encountered while traversing down through children's nodes within any given tree level until every child has been traversed. Every possible path through them has been exhausted before returning up all those values collected along each successive trip into lower depths until they reach childless leaves.

Find the Highest Value in the Tree

To find the highest value in a binary search tree, do the following:

- Find the root of the tree.

- Find the left node.

- Find the right node.

- Look at each branch and compare its value to its parent until you find one with a larger value or until you reach a leaf node, which will contain your answer if there are no branches to explore further!

Find if a Value Exists in the BST Recursively

A recursive solution to this problem calls itself. The idea behind recursion is to define a function to call itself, meaning that the function has at least one reference to itself in its body.

The function does not have to return a value; instead, it may take out information from its environment and store it for future use (i.e., recursion). In our case, we need a stack; we'll use the current node as our stack base and push any nodes from the left or right subtree into our stack (if there are any).

Chapter 12

Red-Black Trees

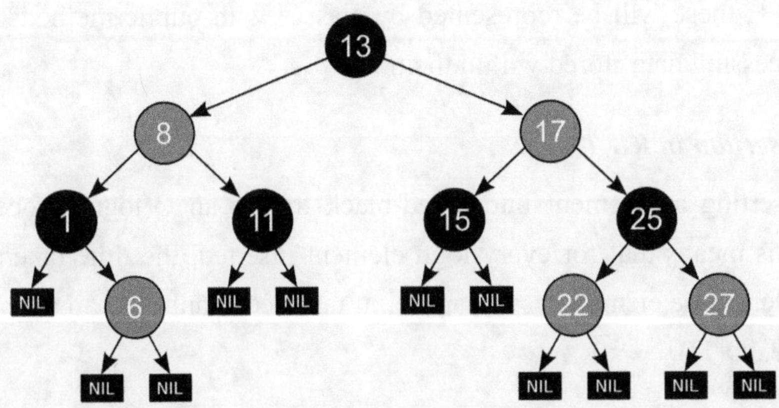

Red-black trees are a self-balancing binary search tree data structure invented by Rudolf Bayer. They are usually implemented using red-black or AVL trees. The distinguishing feature of red-black trees is that they guarantee a minimum degree of balance: each node is either black or red, with exactly one child (either black or red). This property makes it possible to compare elements in the tree and efficiently insert and delete elements from the tree. Red-black trees are used extensively in computer science because they allow for fast searches, even on large datasets.

RB Tree Properties

Red-black trees are self-balancing, meaning that the heights of the two subtrees of a node differ by at most one. The root is always the tallest node (the first red node encountered when going up from an empty tree). Each node has up to two children: either both red or black.

To implement RB trees, we need data structures that can store nodes and their children and pointers that point to those nodes. In C++, these will be represented by classes with public methods for accessing data stored within them.

Insertion in RB Tree

Inserting an element into a red-black tree is an O(logn) process. This means that for every logn element inserted, the time taken to insert these elements is linear, i.e., it takes constant time on average (i.e., O(1)).

In this context, inserting an element means moving it from its current location to its correct position in the RB tree according to red-black tree properties. The steps involved in insertion are:

- The first step is finding out whether there is a violation at all by checking if any node has only black links pointing towards it or not. If so, we update them and mark them as red or black until they become balanced again, forming another violation which we then fix again until we reach a balanced state where no violation exists. Thus no further changes will be made during future iterations since all nodes are now fully updated with their new colors based on how many violations were previously subjected to during previous iterations where multiple violations occurred simultaneously.

- If there aren't any violations, move each node one level closer to its parent until it reaches its root node, which remains unchanged throughout processing. Unless otherwise needed for balancing purposes (this could happen if more than one violation existed simultaneously).

- The final step is to check if there are any violations at all by looking at each node and seeing if it has only black links pointing towards it or not. If so, we update them and mark them as red or black until they become balanced again, forming another violation which we then fix again until we reach a balanced state where no violation exists.

Deletion from RB Tree

In a red-black tree, we first find a node with a minimum key to delete a node with a minimum key. If the node has no children, it is a leaf node and can be deleted. However, if the node has children, then it is an internal (non-leaf) node, and we have to find out if it is possible to delete a non-leaf node by first deleting its children. We will see in this section how we can do that.

Red-black trees are a type of self-balancing binary search tree. A self-balancing binary search tree is a data structure that stores values in its nodes and provides fast access to those values. In addition, it keeps the depth of its branch consistent by balancing the right subtree against the left one when inserting or deleting nodes so that both sides remain roughly the same height.

A red-black tree is one where each node has two colors, and any two adjacent nodes must have different colors (so there are no cycles). Therefore, at most half of all internal nodes (which are either black or red) can have one child on each side; otherwise, it would violate this rule.

Red-black trees are an extension of B-trees, which allow efficient insertions and deletions while maintaining their property of being balanced at all times.

Red-Black Trees Specific Properties

Red-Black trees are an implementation of binary search trees. They are similar to a normal binary search tree, except that they have additional properties:

1. The root is always Black

This property is called the "black root property," and it can be used to locate a node in the tree.

The black root property is only a partial solution, however. It will tell us that the node exists, but it won't tell us where in the tree it is located.

2. Both the left and right children of a red node are black.

- The left and right children of a red node are black.

- The left child is the parent node's first node on the left side. It has no right child as well as no parent (it is itself a root).

- The right child is the first node on the right side of its parent node. It has no left child or parent (it is itself a root).

3. Every path from the root to a leaf has the same number of black nodes.

You might think a red-black tree would be no better than a simple binary search tree. You'd be wrong! For example, every path from the root to the leaf has the same number of black nodes. If the path has an odd number of black nodes, then the left child is black; if it has an even number of black nodes, then the right child is black.

This property allows us to use our memory and processing power optimally: we know that given any particular node in any particular subtree (which we can easily find given its parent). All other nodes in that subtree have an equal distance from their parents and each other (i.e., they are not stored at separate levels). This means that when we wish to use these values for some task—say, sorting them—we do not need to perform any more computations than those required by simply traversing down from their respective ancestors until reaching them (a process known as "bucketing").

4. If a node is red, then its children are black.

The fourth property is that if a node is red, its children are black. This is known as the "left red-black property." It can be used to find the left subtree of a red node and ensure that no black node has two red children. For example, the following algorithm can express this property:

- If the current node is black, return null; //don't bother with this step.

- If there are children on this level (if we haven't reached the bottom), check if they're both black or red. If they don't share any common color, we've found a valid left subtree and return it; else, proceed down one level;

- Otherwise, proceed with normalization as usual.

5. The parent of a red node is black(The converse is not always true)

What happens if we have a white node on the left? This is an interesting question and has many ramifications. We can answer this by using the properties of red and black trees to our advantage. So, we'll start with some definitions:

A Red-Black tree is a binary search tree that satisfies these conditions:

- Every node is colored either red or black

- The root is black (The converse of this statement may not hold)

- All leaf nodes are black (The converse of this statement may not hold)

- Every path from a root to an empty node contains the same number of black nodes

- The parent of a red node is black (The converse is not always true)

6. All the leaf nodes are black

- All the leaf nodes are black

All the leaf nodes in red-black trees are black, which means you can use an O (log n) algorithm to traverse the tree from any node to any other (assuming you know how to find the root). This is because every path from the root to the leaf has the same black nodes.

A simple example for this property would be:

- The root node has two children, both of which are red. The left child's color changes from red (its parent) to gray (its grandparent), while the right child's color remains gray. This makes sense because we want our tree structure to reflect certain data properties. If we had a value stored at some index x in our array and wanted it returned, we might need to search through all possible indexes until we found it. Instead, having a single "gray" index between each pair of consecutive red indexes would give us exactly what we're looking for by ensuring that no two adjacent entries could ever appear at any given place within our original array.

Red-black trees are a special kind of binary search trees with some interesting properties. We have seen that every property is true for this data structure except for one: the parent of a red node may not necessarily be black. This property is called 'Associativity,' It allows us to implement deletes in constant time rather than taking O (log N) as rotations do!

Chapter 13

Data Structures Augmentation

Data structure augmentation is a technique to improve the performance of an algorithm. This can be done by adding more memory or changing the data structure used for storing data. It can also be done by changing parameters like time, space and input size, etc., if none of these options works to achieve better performance.

The process of data structure augmentation is as follows:

1. Identify the bottleneck in the algorithm and make all data structures to use that data

2. Create new data structures that are better than what you already have

3. If possible, create data structures that can handle more data than you need

4. Combine the new data structures with your old ones to make them more efficient

5. Repeat steps 1-4 until you reach a point where there is no more performance improvement

Options and Tradeoffs

Data Structures Augmentation is a way to improve the quality of test data. There are two ways to perform Data Structures Augmentation: manually and automatically. A human performs Manual Data Structure Augmentation. In contrast, automatic Data Structure Augmentation is performed by software that can be run by anyone with access to the appropriate tools and resources.

Manual Data Structure Augmentation lets you choose which data structures should be augmented and how they will be augmented (e.g., adding missing values or perturbing existing ones). Automated techniques use machine learning algorithms on datasets with known ground truth to learn how best to augment the target dataset without knowing anything about your target dataset beforehand!

Code Coverage Metrics

Code coverage metrics are generally used to measure the progress of testing. A good test suite should have high code coverage metrics, which means it can test a large portion of the overall codebase. In addition, measuring code coverage can provide feedback on how well your tests are written and/or whether they need improvement.

Code coverage measures how much of your source code has been executed at least once during testing (i.e., how many lines were traversed). It's important to ensure that all areas of your program are covered by tests so that developers can be confident about the functionality and what isn't being tested. And therefore, it needs additional attention if any changes need making later down that road!

Imports Augmentation

To augment your data structure, you must import a library that supports the augmentation you intend to use. You can import individual classes, functions, or data types from a library by including them in your code like this:

```python
import pylab as plt

plt.plot([1,2])

# Import the module from sklearn import tree

from sklearn import tree =
tree.DecisionTreeClassifier(criterion='entro
py', max_depth=5)
```

After importing the library, you can use its functions and classes just like any other python function or class. For example, this code would create a decision tree classifier to make predictions:

```python
tree =
tree.DecisionTreeClassifier(criterion='entro
py', max_depth=5) tree = tree.fit(Xtrain,
ytrain)

ytest = tree.predict(Xtest)
```

The function fit will train your model and return a classifier object. You can use this classifier to make predictions on new data by calling predict on it with some inputs.

Undefined Types Augmentation

The third type of data structure augmentation is undefined types. This form of data structure augmentation enables you to represent data that is not yet available.

The concept of undefined types has been around in programming languages for decades and has been used in many languages. For example, if you want to store an integer value but don't know what it will be until runtime (with a variable), then you can use an integer variable with the "undefined" keyword in Java:

```
int v = new Integer("undefined");
```

Inheritance Augmentation

Inheritance augmentation is a feature that allows you to extend the functionality of a class by using inheritance. This allows you to create new classes that inherit another class's properties and methods. This is useful if you create an extended version of an existing data structure without modifying its source code or refactoring it into a different class hierarchy.

However, there are some drawbacks to this approach:

- You can't change the base class. If you want to make any changes, you must do it in a separate file and import it into your main file using the import statement.

- You can't inherit multiple classes at once. You must inherit one class at a time by separating them with commas in the class statement.

- You can't inherit classes that are in different packages. Be sure to keep all your classes in the same package.

Data Structures

Data Structures is a set of data types and algorithms used to store and manipulate data. Data structures are used in programming languages to store, organize and manipulate data. For example, an array or list is a type of data structure that can be used for organizing multiple pieces of related information like numbers or strings.

The order in which the elements are stored within this specific type of structure depends on its implementation:

- **Arrays** - elements are stored in sequential memory locations (indexed by numbers).

- **Lists** - elements can be inserted anywhere into the list as its size increases. They're also called dynamic arrays because they're only defined once they're created; they grow by adding new items at both ends until full capacity is reached. Then it starts over again with an empty slot before reaching its last entry point.

Data Structures are an integral part of any programming language, and for a good reason. They allow us to store and manipulate data in a way that's easy to understand and maintain. However, they're not without their flaws: they can be slow or inefficient, they don't always support the features we need them to (e.g., inheritance), and they often impose restrictions on how we access this data (e.g., only through methods defined by their class) which may limit how much flexibility we have when reusing code between projects, etc.

Dynamic Order Statistics

Order statistics are a useful data structure that maintains the kth smallest element in a dynamic array of elements. They are faster than naive implementations and can be used in many places. The implementation is simple, but it can get quite complicated to analyze how quickly it runs.

Dynamic Order Statistics Trees Are Faster Than the Naive Implementation of Order Statistics

Dynamic Order Statistics Trees are a more efficient way to implement order statistics. The naive implementation is O(n^2), but the Dynamic Order Statistics Tree has an O(logn) runtime. With the same size data set, you can run your program much faster using Dynamic Order Statistic trees than the naive implementation.

Dynamic Order Statistics Trees Are Used Everywhere

You might have heard of dynamic arrays—lists or vectors that grow and shrink in size. Dynamic arrays are used for all sorts of things, from simple lists to linked lists and trees. The problem is that there's no easy way to implement these data structures in C++.

That's where dynamic order statistics come in: they provide a general framework for representing any number of objects with an ordering relationship (such as the elements of a linked list).

You Can Use Dynamic Order Statistics in Maps, Graphs, Etc.

Dynamic Order Statistics are used in all kinds of data structures. For example, they can be used to efficiently maintain the kth smallest element in a dynamic array of elements. They have many applications and can be found in maps, graphs, trees, and other data structures.

When you are maintaining the kth smallest element, you need to check each element individually if it is smaller than the current smallest element or not. In this case, we say we do not want an optimal solution but one good enough for our purposes. This means that we do not need or desire an optimal solution and are happy with any good enough solution instead of using more memory or processing power than necessary (memory and processor speed being expensive resources).

A Naive Solution

You can think of the naive solution as maintaining a sorted array. To find the median, we look at the middle element in this sorted array, which takes $O(n)$ time. This is not optimal because if you are working with an unordered set of numbers, then you should be able to find the median in $O(1)$ time instead!

An Update Method

The update method is an interesting algorithm you may use in many places. It is used in maps, graphs, etc. For example, update the kth smallest element in a dynamic array of elements.

Let's say your array looks like this:

```
[10, 20, 30]
```

And you want to replace 20 with 15. You can do this using update by doing:

```
array = [10, 20, 30]

array[-1] = 15
```

And now, the array looks like this:

```
[10, 15, 30]
```

Implementation and Complexity Analysis

Let's look at an example of how to implement Dynamic Order Statistics.

- First, you'll need to build a data structure called an ordered binary tree. This structure should have two special nodes: a root node and its children. The root node has one child and another that points to itself (or is null). The children of the root are left pointing upward and right pointing downward, respectively.

- You can then use recursion to traverse this tree in order from left to right or bottom-up.

- If we want our dynamic order statistic value for item i, we simply search through the tree until we find it; say $x = y + 1$, where y is the current item searched for. We need only keep track of how many times each leaf node has been visited during our search because when they have visited again, they will be counted twice (once on their way down from parent nodes and once on their way back up).

What if we want to know our dynamic order statistic value for item j? This is where recursion comes in. We simply search through the tree until we find it; say $x = y + 1$, where y is the current item being searched for. Again, we need only keep track of how many times each leaf node has been visited during our search because when they have visited again, they will be counted twice (once on their way down from parent nodes and once on their way back up). Once we have the dynamic order statistics, we can easily sort each item in our list.

Optimal Solutions

The optimal solution is the one that minimizes the overall objective function. This means you choose your option based on what will help you achieve your goal most efficiently and effectively.

However, it's important to understand that optimal solutions aren't necessarily the best, most efficient, or practical in every case. There are many different types of problems where that won't be effective, so it's important to choose a model and then find an appropriate solution.

In addition, there isn't only one optimal solution: there can be many! For example, if we're looking at a simple optimization problem where we want to find our way through a maze (and there are no other factors involved), then our options might look something like this:

- Go left

- Go right

- Take the path in the middle

- Go straight ahead

- Don't move at all.

If we were using a simple linear programming model, there would only be one optimal solution: going straight ahead. However, if we were using an evolutionary algorithm, many different options could result in a high score.

And we would have many different options available to us. For example, we could go straight ahead and then take a right at the first intersection, or we could go straight ahead and then take a left at the first intersection. That would be an optimal solution if we were using a linear programming model; however, it wouldn't necessarily be one of them when using an evolutionary algorithm.

Applications and Related Problems

Applications of dynamic order statistics include:

- **Data mining**. Dynamic order statistics are used in several algorithms for clustering, recommender systems, and novelty detection. In particular, they can be employed to find the best model parameters or fit within a specific search space that results in the highest quality model. This can be done by searching over different orders of objects to determine which order has the highest likelihood of revealing useful patterns or clusters.

- **Range minimum query (RQ)**. RQ is one of many data mining algorithms that uses dynamic order statistics to cluster objects into groups based on their similarity concerning certain attributes or features. This technique enables it to find clusters as efficiently as possible while still being able to classify new objects quickly and efficiently without having prior knowledge about those items' characteristics other than their relative position within each group (which changes over time).

Chapter 14

Dynamic Programming

Dynamic programming is a general algorithm design technique. It works by breaking down complex problems into smaller subproblems and combining solutions to these subproblems. In this way, dynamic programming can be used as a time-space tradeoff. Solving more of the smaller subproblems takes less time than solving the larger problem directly. Still, it uses more memory space than other approaches that solve only one instance of the problem at hand (such as memorization). In some cases, dynamic programming can even eliminate redundant computations by combining solutions from multiple instances of the same problem into one big solution simultaneously!

Dynamic programming is a technique used in many fields to solve optimization problems. In its simplest form, dynamic programming is a greedy algorithm that uses recursion and memorization to speed up solutions to problems with optimal substructure. Dynamic programming can be applied to any problem where the optimal solution can be broken down into smaller subproblems that are similar or identical.

The Value of Subproblems

The value of a subproblem is the minimum of all values for that subproblem and all other subproblems. In other words, it's the least amount you can get by solving every problem as if it were an optimization problem.

For example, consider this problem: You have five coins whose values add up to $2.25. How many ways are there to make change for $3? There are two solutions: use one or four coins; in either case, you'll get $1 in change (plus some extra pennies). So, if your objective function says, "get at least $1 in change," you've already found one solution: [1]! But what if we wanted more than just one solution? For example, maybe we wanted to find as many different solutions as possible so we could see how much variety there was between them—and also so we could count how many possibilities there were overall. So, we'd have to write our function differently now: instead of saying "get at least 1 dollar back," we'd say "get at least 1 dollar back from using any combination of 5 coins." This way, the objective function would return the minimum number of ways through which our initial set can be partitioned into groups. Each group would have exactly 1 coin worth at least 1 dollar left after taking away all but one coin from each group (so that when we consolidate these groups together again later on).

A Recursive Solution

Recursive solutions are a type of dynamic programming solution. This means that you have to solve a problem in two phases:

- Solve the problem for the initial state, which is given as a seed value.

- Use this solution as an input to your recursive function, then iterate until you reach some termination condition (i.e., when no more values are left).

A Memorized Solution

Memorization is a time-space tradeoff. In other words, it's a technique that allows us to avoid recalculating the same results repeatedly by storing them in a table so that we can just look up the answer without calculating it every time. This can have significant performance benefits when you have many subproblems that are similar and take too long to solve each time they're encountered.

The memorized solution uses a table named _memoization_table (or something like that) to store the results of subproblems, which means we need some way of generating unique keys for each element in our table, so they don't get confused with one another.

We'll use our index as an example:

We'll first create a function that will use our index as the key and return the value stored under that key. We'll call it lookup value and make it take an array of keys as its only argument:

def lookup_value(keys): If we call this function with a list of keys as an argument, it will return the value stored under that key

Top-Down vs. Bottom-Up

There are two main solutions to dynamic programming problems:

- Top-down

- Bottom-up

The top-down solution is recursive and uses the concept of recursion (a function calling itself). The bottom-up approach uses memorization, which means storing the results of previous computations to avoid repeating them.

Dynamic Programming Is a Time-Space Tradeoff

Dynamic Programming is a time-space tradeoff. It's a technique for solving problems by breaking them down into subproblems, computing solutions to each subproblem, and storing the results in a table. The solution to the original problem can then be found by querying this table. Dynamic programming is useful when you have many different ways of thinking about a problem but only need one answer (which may be used repeatedly). This often happens in computer science because computers are so fast at doing repetitive tasks that it makes sense to use them, even if it means sacrificing space.

Dynamic Programming is a powerful technique that can be applied to many problems. We've shown how it can be used to solve the bin packing problem, which we saw has applications in supply chain management, but there are many other possible applications.

Dynamic Programming is also used in various areas, including economics, game theory, AI planning agents, and more!

Elements of Dynamic Programming

Dynamic programming is an approach to solving a problem that involves breaking it down into smaller subproblems and then solving each subproblem. The result is that when you go back to the original problem, you already have an optimal solution ready to go.

Optimal Sub-Structure

The optimal substructure property of dynamic programming states that if you have an optimal solution for a problem and find a subproblem with the same optimal solution, then you can use the answer to your sub-problem to solve your original problem.

The next step is to apply this idea to our matrix multiplication example. We've already figured out how many products we need to create, and we know that once a product has been created, it will be used in almost every other product (i.e., no duplicates). So now we need only look at the values in each row across all five matrices. When this is done, we'll see that every one of these numbers is either 0 or 1!

This means there are only two types of products: ones made by multiplying two matrices together (these are denoted as matrix products) and ones made by multiplying one matrix against itself (these are called triangular products). Suppose we work backward through our algorithm from here on out using these new rules instead of just looking for ways to reuse values across multiple rows like before. In that case, our job becomes much simpler because there aren't longer any duplicate products being created!

Overlapping Sub-Problems

As you may have guessed from reading the previous section, there are two different types of overlapping sub-problems:

- Sub-problem A is used in multiple sub-problems. For example:

```java
int a = 3;

int find_area(int x, int y) { return x * y;
}

int find_area(int x, int y) { return x * y +
1; }
```

This problem has one overlapping sub-problem: `find_area(x,y).` It's used twice in this program (once as `a` and once as `b`). If we want to solve all three instances of `find_area,` we could just call it once and pass in the values from each line. The first time through would look like this:

```java
`java public static void main(String[]
args) { System. out. println("Area 0");
System.out.println("a = " + a);
System.out.println("b = " + b); area0();
}
```

In our case here, though, we don't have any other problems that use this method, so we won't need to repeat it here--we just need one instance for both lines above!

Memoization

Memoization is a technique to speed up the process. Let's say you want to find the value of n!, which is the product of all integers from 1 to n. You could use dynamic programming for this problem, but it would be pretty slow because you have a lot of sub-problems that are similar to each other:

```
$$n! = \sum_{i=1}^{n}i$$ or
$$\frac{2}{3}\cdot\frac{4}{5}\cdot\frac{6}{7
}\cdot...\cdot (2)(3)(4)...(n)\dots $$ where
$n$ is the number being computed.
```

The trick here is that we already know how many times each factorial will appear in our formula. So we can just save ourselves some time by not computing them again if they're already stored elsewhere!

Tabulation

The process of tabulation is the act of storing intermediate results in a table. Tabulation is useful for problems that have overlapping sub-problems, as we see in dynamic programming problems. In dynamic programming, we can use tabulation to store values from our current iteration over time to make decisions later on when it comes time to choose what action to take next.

Learning About Dynamic Programming Is Good for Understanding How to Use It

The first thing you should know about dynamic programming is that it can be used to solve problems in many different fields. The technique was first discovered by Richard Bellman and Albert W. Tucker, who tried solving a problem related to control theory in aerospace engineering. But since then, dynamic programming has been used to solve problems in economics, artificial intelligence, operations research, and many other fields!

Here's how it works: Dynamic programming is a general method for solving a problem by breaking it down into subproblems — smaller versions of your original problem — and then solving each subproblem separately before combining all of their solutions into one final solution for your original problem. This approach allows us to solve complicated problems more efficiently by working backward from the final results we want instead of forwards from the beginning of our calculations.

Both the theory and practice of dynamic programming are fascinating. It's a powerful tool that can solve many problems more efficiently, but it also helps us understand how to improve our algorithms and find better solutions for any problem.

Chapter 15

Greedy Algorithms

Greedy algorithms are simple. They are shortsighted in their approach to problem-solving. They take the best immediate or local solution while finding an answer. The main focus of greedy algorithms is making the optimal choice at that given moment. This is one of the main reasons greedy algorithms aren't used for more complex problems. They don't tend to look at the bigger picture. Greedy Algorithms will make what looks to be the optimal choice based on current information but may not yield an overall optimal solution. It's important that you can determine if a problem can be solved using a greedy approach because then you have a great strategy for going about solving that problem step-wise."

Greedy Algorithms Are Simple. They Are Shortsighted in Their Approach to Problem-Solving. They Take the Best Immediate or Local Solution While Finding an Answer

For example: If you were on a diet and wanted to lose 10 pounds, you could choose a greedy approach and eat less food than usual for three days straight (or even just one day). This would be a great way to start losing weight immediately—but it's not necessarily the most effective long-term strategy. Suppose you exercise every day instead of binging on snacks late at night while watching TV all weekend long. In that case, your body composition might change slowly but result in better overall health than if you'd gone with the temporary "easy fix."

The Main Focus of Greedy Algorithms Is Making the Optimal Choice at That Given Moment. This Is One of The Main Reasons Greedy Algorithms Aren't Used for More Complex Problems. They Don't Tend to Look at the Bigger Picture

In contrast, dynamic programming algorithms consider future consequences, leading to better solutions. A good example of this is in chess: if you are playing black and want to take white's rook on the third rank, it will be tempting to play your pawn forward because it looks like a good move now. However, if you do this, then white will be able to capture your queen by moving their knight around behind your king! So, although moving your pawn forward may seem like an idea at first glance, it sets up white for an easy win!

Greedy Algorithms Will Make What Looks to Be the Optimal Choice Based on Current Information But May Not Yield an Overall Optimal Solution

You can think of greedy algorithms as being more like someone who makes decisions based on their immediate needs and wants rather than someone who has a longer-term plan in mind that considers all possible outcomes of each decision. For example, if you were making dinner plans with your friend tonight and wanted them to pick where we eat, they might ask you what type of food you want—and say something like "I want pizza!" or "I want Chinese!" And you'd reply with something like: "Well then, I guess we're going for pizza?" or "Let's order Chinese then." You've just used a greedy algorithm!

It's Important for You to Determine If a Problem Can Be Solved Using a Greedy Approach Because Then You Have a Great Strategy for Going about Solving That Problem Step-Wise

The next step is determining if the problem can be solved using a greedy approach. It's important to know if this is true because then you have a great strategy for how to go about solving that problem in a step-wise fashion.

If your problem has multiple solutions, greediness won't be helpful because there are many different ways of getting from point A to point B - and some may not even resemble each other much! On the other hand, if you don't want every possible solution but want one that works well for you, then greediness might still work for you. But only if it's clear which solution is "best."

An Example of a Problem That Can Be Solved Using This Method Is Scheduling Activities with Certain Start and Ending Times and Picking Which Activities to Do First to Accomplish as Many Tasks as Possible

You can use Greedy Algorithms to solve many small and large problems. An example of a problem that can be solved using this method is scheduling activities with certain start and ending times and picking which activities to do first to accomplish as many tasks as possible.

You can also use Greedy Algorithms to solve problems where you have a list of items that need to be processed. For example, cleaning all the dishes before doing other chores around the house could be considered a Greedy Algorithm problem. Because every time you wash one dish, you're going through your list of chores until it's empty again. This will change depending on what order you do things in, though (e.g., washing all cups first, then pans), making it harder than just picking something randomly from your entire list!

Greedy Algorithms Aren't Always the Best Way to Solve Problems, But If You Think They'll Work for Your Situation, You Should Probably Try Them Out First

Greedy algorithms are simple. They are shortsighted in their approach to problem-solving. They take the best immediate or local solution while finding an answer. The main focus of greedy algorithms is making the optimal choice at that given moment. For example, the greedy algorithm would be the best choice if you want to get from point A to point B as fast as possible. It focuses on getting there as fast as possible without wasting time thinking about paths that may take longer but include less traffic or roads with better terrain (like going across a bridge instead of driving through a swamp).

Greedy algorithms work well for many problems where your goal is to find an optimal solution—or at least one that satisfies some constraint like maximum profit or minimum cost. But they aren't always appropriate. Sometimes, we need our algorithm's behavior to depend on the information that wasn't available at its creation time (for example, when estimating future prices based on past data).

Elements of the Greedy Strategy

The greedy approach is a greedy algorithm that tries to minimize the cost of a problem by performing locally optimal actions. The greedy approach is not always the best way to solve a problem, but it can be very effective in many cases.

The greedy approach is a greedy algorithm, an optimization technique that uses suboptimal information to find the best solution to a problem. A greedy algorithm operates by choosing the best option from each choice at its disposal. So, for example, if you're trying to find the fastest way through traffic, you could choose to go straight instead of taking your normal route through residential streets because it would likely be faster than driving around in circles for 20 minutes looking for parking on a Saturday afternoon.

The greedy algorithm finds solutions by making small sacrifices (weighted according to relative importance) to achieve an overall goal or objective. This strategy can also be used with other types of algorithms like neural networks--where elements are arranged based on proximity rather than priority--to improve accuracy while reducing cost or time required for calculations."

Selection of Variable

After identifying the variable, you have to decide on which of its values is considered more valuable. There are four different ways to approach this:

- **Select the variable with the highest value (or maximum).** The primary benefit of this strategy is that it requires no additional steps. Therefore it's often used in a hurry or when the user interface doesn't allow for much customization. However, it may not accurately reflect what's needed by your business. For example, if you're optimizing for a conversion metric but don't want to drive up prices too far above your competitors' offers, selecting the maximum value isn't work very well. Because it will likely lead you down an entirely different path than if we were optimizing for revenue instead — think about how much money people would spend if their only concern were maximizing profit!

- **Select the variable with the lowest value (or minimum).** This strategy is most useful when more than two variables are involved in determining what action should be taken next (like looking at three items on sale at various prices). Because then we can prioritize which one needs attention first based on which one has less effective overall. So, if all three items together would bring us $100 worth of profit per sale while only selling two out of three total would still make us $50 each time we sold two out of three times, then choosing not to buy any items might be best. Think how much better off our company could be without spending any extra cash upfront just yet! But remember: Your goal here isn't necessarily sustainability - sometimes being profitable means spending more money upfront until later when those investments pay off big dividends! Make sure whatever course of action ultimately chosen makes sense from both perspectives before deciding whether or not one option represents greater potential success than another."

Validity of Operation and Assignment of Value

You must also consider the validity of operation and assignment of value. Validity of operation refers to the ability of the strategy to work. In this case, every member in a given environment can implement it without fail. Assignment of value refers to how much each member earns based on their role within the group's operations. For example, if we were trying to form a new club at school, and five students wanted to join:

- One president

- Two vice presidents

- One secretary-treasurer (or treasurer)

- One assistant treasurer (or treasurer)

One problem with our new club would be whether or not members could do their jobs properly. For example, would people know how many kids were interested in joining? Would they have enough money saved up for dues payments? Would they know what events to hold during meetings to get more participants involved? If these questions weren't answered first before starting any kind of organization, then it wouldn't have any chance of being successful later down the line because its leaders wouldn't know what kind

of direction, need to occur before starting activities related directly towards gaining popularity among potential recruits."

Objective Function

The objective function is the mathematical measure of performance for a decision-making problem. It is a function (or relationship) between the variables of the problem and its solution, such as "how many units of each product should be made?" or "what should my salary be?"

The objective function takes into consideration any factors that are being optimized by your algorithm. When it comes to greedy algorithms, there's only one factor to optimize: how much money you make. As such, your goal will be to maximize that amount by choosing what products you offer at what prices—and no matter what happens in life (like getting fired), this remains true.

In the Greedy Set Cover Problem, Optimal Substructure and Greedy Choice Property Occur

A greedy strategy is a heuristic algorithm that assigns one task at a time and chooses the best available option. Of course, this algorithm doesn't always find the optimal solution, but it does work well in many cases.

In the greedy set cover problem, you select tasks one by one and choose the better option until all tasks are covered. Of course, there's no guarantee this will be an optimal solution, nor is there any guarantee that your chosen task assignments can be reached since they're just guesses at what might be best until all information has been gathered. However, suppose you start with low-ranking tasks first and continue in order of decreasing value to each task type (you may have already noticed this trend in our code). In that case, your choices will likely become increasingly optimal because higher-ranking items tend not to remain unassigned for long periods before being picked up by someone else or needing attention.

The greedy approach is used to solve the problem of set cover. The greedy approach is one of the most simple and efficient algorithms. It has been successfully applied in many applications with good results.

Conclusion

If you want to start grokking algorithms, this book is for you. It is a detailed guide to understanding the world of complex mathematical computations. This book will help you better understand how algorithms work and how to apply them effectively in your daily life.

References

Anderson, Ross C, Meg Guerreiro, and Joanna Smith. 2016. "Are all biases bad? Collaborative grounded theory in developmental evaluation of education policy." Journal of Multidisciplinary Evaluation 12 (27):44-57.

Creswell, John W, and Cheryl N Poth. 2017. Qualitative inquiry and research design: Choosing among five approaches: Sage publications.

Miles, Matthew B., and Michael A. Huberman. 1994. Qualitative Data Analysis. 2nd edition ed. Thousand Oaks, CA.: Sage

Sinkovics, Rudolf R., Elfriede Penz, and Pervez N. Ghauri. 2008. "Enhancing the Trustworthiness of Qualitative Research in International Business." Management International Review 48 (6):689-714. doi: 10.1007/s11575-008-0103-z.

Alvesson, Mats, and Dan Kärreman. 2007. "Constructing mystery: Empirical matters in theory development." Academy of management review 32 (4):1265-1281.

Miles, Matthew B, A Michael Huberman, and Johnny Saldana. 2013. Qualitative data analysis: A methods sourcebook. Thousand Oaks, CA: SAGE Publications, Incorporated. 26